There was a man named Elkanah
who lived in Ramah in the region of
Zuph in the hill country of Ephraim.
He was the son of Jeroham, son of Elihu,
son of Tohu, son of Zuph, of Ephraim.
Elkanah had two wives, Hannah and
Peninnah. Peninnah had children,
but Hannah did not.

—1 Samuel 1:1–2 (NLT)

Extraordinary Women OF THE BIBLE

HIGHLY FAVORED: MARY'S STORY

SINS AS SCARLET: RAHAB'S STORY

A HARVEST OF GRACE: RUTH AND NAOMI'S STORY

AT HIS FEET: MARY MAGDALENE'S STORY

TENDER MERCIES: ELIZABETH'S STORY

WOMAN OF REDEMPTION: BATHSHEBA'S STORY

JEWEL OF PERSIA: ESTHER'S STORY

A HEART RESTORED: MICHAL'S STORY

BEAUTY'S SURRENDER: SARAH'S STORY

THE WOMAN WARRIOR: DEBORAH'S STORY

THE GOD WHO SEES: HAGAR'S STORY

THE FIRST DAUGHTER: EVE'S STORY

THE ONES JESUS LOVED: MARY AND MARTHA'S STORY

THE BEGINNING OF WISDOM: BILQIS'S STORY

THE SHADOW'S SONG: MAHLAH AND NO'AH'S STORY

DAYS OF AWE: EUODIA AND SYNTYCHE'S STORY

BELOVED BRIDE: RACHEL'S STORY

A PROMISE FULFILLED: HANNAH'S STORY

Extraordinary Women OF THE BIBLE

A PROMISE
FULFILLED

HANNAH'S STORY

Tricia Goyer

 Guideposts

Extraordinary Women of the Bible is a trademark of Guideposts.

Published by Guideposts
100 Reserve Road, Suite E200
Danbury, CT 06810
Guideposts.org

This is a work of fiction. While the characters and settings are drawn from scripture references and historical accounts, apart from the actual people, events, and locales that figure into the fiction narrative, all other names, characters, places, and events are the creation of the author's imagination or are used fictitiously.

Every attempt has been made to credit the sources of copyrighted material used in this book. If any such acknowledgment has been inadvertently omitted or miscredited, receipt of such information would be appreciated.

Scripture references are from the following sources: The Holy Bible, King James Version (KJV). New American Standard Bible (NASB). Copyright © 1960, 1962, 1963, 1968, 1971, 1972, 1973, 1975, 1977, 1995 by the Lockman Foundation. Used by permission. The Holy Bible, New International Version (NIV). Copyright © 1973, 1978, 1984, 2011 by Biblica, Inc. Used by permission of Zondervan. All rights reserved worldwide. www.zondervan.com. Holy Bible, New Living Translation (NLT). Copyright © 1996. Used by permission of Tyndale House Publishers, Inc., Wheaton, Illinois 60189. All rights reserved.

Cover and interior design by Müllerhaus
Cover illustration by Brian Call represented by Illustration Online LLC.
Typeset by Aptara, Inc.

ISBN 978-1-961126-74-9 (hardcover)
ISBN 978-1-961126-75-6 (epub)

Printed and bound in the United States of America
10 9 8 7 6 5 4 3 2 1

Extraordinary Women OF THE BIBLE

A PROMISE
FULFILLED

HANNAH'S STORY

DEDICATION

To my mother, Linda Martina, whose strength and
grace echo the timeless spirit of Hannah. Your enduring love
and faith have been a guiding light, pointing me to
God's goodness. Thank you.

ACKNOWLEDGMENTS

First and foremost, a heartfelt thanks to Michelle, my cohost for the Daily Bible Podcast. Diving into God's Word with you has been a transformative journey and a deep source of joy. To our listeners of the Daily Bible Podcast: your passion and commitment inspire me daily to delve deeper into God's Word and to understand His people better—thank you for being the fuel to this fire.

I want to extend my deepest gratitude to Janet Grant, a remarkable agent whose belief in my writing career never wavered and who stood steadfastly by my side. To the incredibly talented editorial team at Guideposts: Your meticulous attention to detail, insights, and unwavering dedication transformed this manuscript into the masterpiece it is today. Your patience and guidance have been invaluable, and I'm eternally grateful.

Lastly, to my cherished grandmother, Dolores Coulter: your legacy of trust in prayer and unshakable faith in God's plan has left an indelible mark on my heart. This book is not only a reflection of the lessons you've imparted but also a tribute to your enduring faith.

Cast of
CHARACTERS

Hannah • mother of Samuel, first wife to Elkanah
Elkanah • father of Samuel, husband to Hannah and Peninnah
Peninnah • second wife of Elkanah

ELKANAH & PENINNAH'S CHILDREN:
Ayala • the firstborn child and oldest daughter, wife to Simeon
Eitan • the second-born child and oldest son
Oren • the third-born child and second oldest son
Abiram • the fourth-born child and third oldest son
Zemir • the fifth-born child and fourth oldest son
Ya'akov • the sixth-born child and fifth oldest son
Leeba • the seventh-born child and youngest daughter
Tobiah • the eighth-born child and sixth youngest son

Adi • one of Peninnah's servant girls
Deborah • midwife
Eli • high priest
Hophni • Eli's son
Phinehas • Eli's son
Rina • choir leader and wife of a Levite
Ruth • her daughter violated by Eli's sons
Shifrah • a servant of Elkanah and Hannah
Simeon • Ayala's husband
Yonah • one of the women from Hannah's community

Glossary of
TERMS

abba • father

Asherah • goddess of the sea and wife of El

Baal • the Canaanite god of weather, believed to control the fertility of crops, animals, and people

charoset • sweet paste made of fruits and nuts, eaten at the Passover Seder

Chemosh • savage war god

doda • aunt

Feast of Unleavened Bread • a time of remembrance and reflection on Yahweh's deliverance from the land of Egypt

imma • mother

maror • bitter herbs eaten at Passover

Shavuot • the Festival of Weeks, held seven weeks after Passover, marks the giving of the Torah at Mount Sinai

Sukkot • the Festival of Booths

CHAPTER ONE

Hannah sat on an aged tree stump and glanced over her shoulder at the thickly foliaged woods, always watchful, always listening. As a child, her strongest memory was of the day the prisoner-turned-victor Samson demolished a thousand of the Philistine elite, along with their temple. Such a celebration she hadn't witnessed before or since. Filled with Yahweh-given power, Samson had crushed their enemies, and her people had lived in peace for a time. But no longer. The sons of the slain men had grown and now plagued the hill country of Ephraim and beyond. Peace eluded her community, and so had Hannah's most desired dream of becoming a wife and a mother. A wife, yes, but even after ten years of marriage, no children had come.

For the first three years, Hannah had clung to hope. Then her husband chose to take another wife—and Hannah could not blame him. What Israelite man did not want a son or a dozen of them? Yet when Peninnah conceived within the first few months, Hannah's fears were confirmed. She herself was the problem. Month by month, she dared to hope for a child, but as the years slipped by, Hannah's hope was washed away with rivers of tears and replaced with a deep pool of self-blame.

Tears again spilled onto the stump's bark, rough and weathered beneath her.

Yahweh, what have I done to forsake You? Why do You make me as barren as this stump? If I only knew what would please You, I would change. Please, tell me what You require. I will be quick to obey.

Hannah wiped her cheeks and inhaled the cool, misty fragrance of the brook. The damp scent of water blended with the tangy smell of moss-covered stones and the sweet fragrance of wildflowers. Even this peaceful place could not erase the pain inside. Knotted inside Hannah's chest, her heart had grown as hard as the pebble-strewn creek bed beneath the flowing water. Outwardly, she portrayed herself as the meek wife who trusted wholeheartedly in Yahweh. But inwardly she was boiling with questions and doubt. When least expected, despair crept in as an unwelcome enemy. Would she be able to keep it at bay? Or would this invisible enemy kidnap her soul, forever pulling her into a dark abyss?

She clung to the slightest hope that Yahweh had not wholly forsaken her. And in the heart of the dense forest near Ramathaim-Zophim, she dared to hope she would be safe here too. Though the danger of another Philistine attack was ever present, in the last few years, Hannah nevertheless chose to fill her waterskins alone.

The other women, with their servants and children in tow, gathered their water downstream, close to town. She imagined their chatter and laughter. Laughter that would die down as she neared. Although the community respected the wife of one of the leading Levite teachers and tabernacle musicians, Hannah was excluded from their close-knit circles. Perhaps they too believed her to be cursed? Or perhaps they felt guilty as they celebrated their ever-growing families while she remained childless?

Hannah sighed. Their pity was as piercing as the empty space within. She placed a hand on her flat stomach and then shook her head. Allowing her thoughts to linger on her pain would help nothing. It only stripped away every ounce of strength, causing her to retreat to her bed.

Then, at those times, she was both barren and useless. At least she could do her part to comfort Elkanah after a long day's work and assist her husband's second wife in caring for the children.

Hannah knew that her childlessness weighed heavily on Elkanah, though he never once spoke a word of reproach. His faith in Yahweh was a pillar of strength for both of them, especially during these turbulent times when devout followers were few.

Today, she needed at least a few more minutes to wrestle with her thoughts and pray. Sunbeams peeped through the leafy canopy, casting patterns of light and shade across her. After a few more deep breaths and whispered prayers, she stood and brushed a dry leaf from her homespun garment.

Hannah's slender fingers worked methodically as she filled the first of two waterskins. The damp moss that crept around the bank's edge lent a soft, velvety contrast to the crisp, cool water, which danced in the dappled sunlight. The chatter of the brook attempted to lull her to believe she was not being foolish to come here alone. But in her heart she knew, despite her hopes and prayers, there was no such thing as safety in the hill country of Ephraim these days.

Attempting to push away the weight of worries, Hannah squared her shoulders and jutted out her chin, sealed the first waterskin, and took up the second. She would have to hurry. Soon Elkanah would return from the music lesson he was giving his oldest nephews. As the youngest of Jeroham's sons, Elkanah was only five or six years older than his nephews. He enjoyed playful banter with the young men—until the music lessons began. Once the harp or lyre was in hand, Elkanah transformed before them into a dedicated, priestly musician who led his fellow Levites through the traditional songs that accompanied the Lord's holy days. Hannah dipped the second waterskin into the creek, remembering how she used to imagine her husband teaching the same songs to their—

A bird's caw broke through her thoughts. A second caw sounded—a warning—and Hannah's eyes widened. Did Philistine warriors approach? She hurriedly sealed the waterskin. Her senses heightened and her heart pounded.

The noise of footsteps filled the quiet forest. Hannah slung both waterskins over her shoulder and hoisted her skirt, preparing to run. Her breath caught at the flash of gray clothing in the woods. A dark-haired person, head down. Hannah planted her foot to run in the opposite direction when the person's size and features came into focus. Not those of a Philistine but of a child. The small figure stumbled out of the dense undergrowth, racing toward her. Hannah knew her. Ayala.

The child's eyes were wide, and tears streamed down her cheeks. Her dress, vibrant blue when Hannah saw her this morning, was now mottled with dirt and leaf stains. The gray clothing Hannah had spotted moments ago was a too-large cloak hanging off her tiny shoulders—no doubt borrowed from one of their servants to help with her escape from the cluster of families gathered at the main watering hole.

Hannah's heart clenched at the sight. She slid the water-skins off her shoulder and onto the ground.

"Ayala!" Hannah extended a hand. "I am here. Come, child." She took a deep breath and tried to hide the frustration that rippled from her pounding heart like grains of wheat slipping through a split sack.

Ayala stilled. Her wide eyes flickered from Hannah's extended hand to her face. Beneath the girl's fear—probably warranted, as she would be reprimanded for leaving the group—there was also a desperate glimmer of hope. Hope that she would be seen, acknowledged. Peninnah's oldest, with four younger brothers, Ayala often turned to Hannah for comfort or attention, yet she had never gone to such great lengths to receive either.

"I found you." Ayala's voice escaped between pants.

A shiver raced down Hannah's spine, thinking of what horrible things could have happened if Ayala had not found her. The muscles in Hannah's neck tightened, and her stomach did a flip. Surely there was a reason Ayala sought her out.

"And why were you looking?" Hannah waited, her hand still outstretched.

Ayala came closer and lowered her head. "I dropped my bread. One of the stray dogs snatched it. I wanted more, but when I tried to tell *Imma*, she yelled at me. I saw you leaving the path, coming here...." Ayala wrapped the cloak tighter around herself. "I just borrowed this. I will take it back. No one saw me go."

Hannah's heart tightened with realization. If she had unwittingly led Ayala away from the group and the Philistines attacked... The danger she might have unknowingly exposed the girl to weighed on her. But Hannah quickly pushed those thoughts away, taking another deep breath. The Lord was watching over them—protecting them both.

Hannah *had* needed a time of solitude and prayer away from the others, especially the ever-watchful gaze of Elkanah's second wife. Ayala's mother was as nosy as she was beautiful. Hannah had no doubt she would return from the gathering commenting about every other woman in their community, and she'd prattle on until Elkanah finished his lessons and returned home. Elkanah chose to ignore the judgmental side of the younger woman. Then again, he often did not witness how Peninnah mocked Hannah or ignored Ayala in favor of tending to her sons.

Ayala hurled herself into Hannah's arms with a soft cry. Hannah encased her in a firm, protective hold.

Ayala's body trembled. "I saw you leave. I wanted to come. I—"

Hannah offered a quick embrace then pulled back and stood. No matter how much she longed to comfort the girl and say that she understood, Hannah could not. *Would not.* This was not her child. Whatever fault Yahweh found in her, she would not add to His displeasure by bringing division between mother and child.

Hannah's lips pressed together in a tight line. She retrieved her waterskins, slung them over her shoulder, and took the girl's small hand in hers. "We need to return. I will take you to your imma."

"I want to be with you," Ayala cried. She pulled her hand from Hannah's grasp and flung her arms around Hannah's waist.

Empathy welled up in Hannah's heart. Gently, she loosened Ayala's grip and held the girl's tear-soaked face in her hands.

"Imma is caring for the boys," Ayala said, pouting. "She does not even know I left."

"You are nearly six, and you do not need the same attention as your brothers, dear one," Hannah murmured, her voice a soft lullaby of consolation. "We will go together to find your imma. She must be worried sick about you."

Yet the words had barely exited Hannah's mouth when a sound caused them both to jump.

The forest seemed to close around them. Footsteps, growing nearer. Fear coursed through Hannah's veins. Ayala clung to her.

"Is it the bad men?" Ayala whispered. "Or could it be my imma?"

Hannah paused, her gaze vacillating between Ayala and the direction the sounds were coming from.

The fear of falling into Philistine hands outweighed worries about another confrontation with Peninnah. A wave of relief washed over Hannah as Elkanah emerged from the forest's edge. Although he was a Levite, he was not in his priestly robes now. Instead, he wore his simple tunic of rough-spun fabric, the color of freshly turned soil. Elkanah looked handsome and reliable, as he always did to Hannah. But why was he here and not at his lessons?

His eyes widened under dark brows when he spotted her. Yet he did not seem surprised to see Ayala at her side. "Hannah! Why are you here, wandering so far from home?" His gaze fell first to the waterskin and then to his daughter. "And it seems someone is learning your unwise ways," Elkanah admonished, warily scanning the surrounding woods.

Her husband's voice resonated with a mixture of irritation and concern. Yet beneath it all, Hannah knew the depths of his affection and protective instincts. Her heart was a tangle of regret and appreciation as she met Elkanah's gaze. His reprimand stemmed from his concern for her. Even though she'd given him no children, Elkanah loved her well. His feelings were visible in the worry lines etched on his forehead and the tenderness in his gaze.

"I am sorry, Elkanah," she murmured, emotion catching in her throat. "I simply wanted time away to think. To pray." Her eyelashes fluttered closed. She did not need to tell him what she'd prayed for—she knew her husband prayed the same.

Instinctively her hand touched her flat stomach, as it so often did. Elkanah's expression softened, his eyes brimming with compassion. He extended his hand, gently brushing a stray lock of hair behind Hannah's ear.

"I understand, my love," he murmured. His touch lingered on her face. But his own face held shadows of worries and concerns beyond this moment.

"Elkanah, what troubles you?" Hannah reached out and took his hand, feeling the warmth of his strong fingers.

He sighed, his brow furrowing. "It is our people. I see them straying farther from Yahweh's path every day. On the way to find you, I noticed another pagan altar was set up. Some have begun to worship false idols."

"But why did you come to find me now? Why are you not at the lessons?"

"A messenger arrived." Elkanah's voice dropped to an even more serious tone. "The Philistines are on the move. There is talk of unrest, perhaps even conflict." Worry etched deeper into the lines of her husband's face, and she could see his shoulders tense.

Hannah's heart raced in her chest, the weight of his words pulling her from her personal sorrow. *Enemies from within their tribe. And from beyond their borders. The first causing the devout to stray. The second to steal and to kill.* Thoughts of the Philistines' invasions long ago made her stomach clench.

"The Philistines?" A chill ran down her spine. "What does this mean for us, for our village?"

"I do not know yet. But we must be vigilant. We must pray for wisdom and strength and for protection from foreign enemies and our people who wish to seek other gods." Elkanah sighed. "The Lord will guide us."

A surge of warmth flooded her. "I am truly sorry that I was followed."

"I understand why the little lamb came to find you. You are gentle and safe." Elkanah enveloped Hannah in his arms, pulling her into a protective hug. "I am fortunate to have you by my side, and I pledge always to shield and bolster you. I understand you need time away. Still..." Then, just as quickly as he embraced her, he stepped back. "We cannot tarry. I must take the news to the others."

She nodded and peered down at Ayala. Her eyes flashed with uncertainty. Her lips were slightly parted as if poised to voice a question. Hannah grasped her hand and urged her forward as she moved to join Elkanah.

When they reached the road leading to the village, Hannah waved her husband ahead. "Go, tell the others. We will go straight home, I promise."

As they walked, Ayala glanced up at Hannah. "My *abba*... he does not show such love to my *imma*," she murmured, studying Hannah's face for answers.

Hannah felt a pang of sorrow for the innocent girl. How could she explain? "Each relationship is unique." Hannah forced a smile. "Love shows itself in various ways, and sometimes it can be hard to comprehend."

Ayala nodded, her forehead wrinkling, still clearly unsure.

"I am here for you, Ayala." Hannah squeezed the girl's hand. "Whenever you need someone to talk to, remember that."

Ayala's eyes lit with hope.

"We must hurry home, dear one." Hannah forced a smile, trying to hide her concern.

Ahead, the village of Ramathaim-Zophim, usually so comforting in its familiarity, seemed to vibrate with tension. The loamy smell of the nearby fields was tainted with the feeling that formidable foes would soon emerge from the town's forests. Down on the plains, their enemy fought with chariots. But in the hills of Ephraim, the chariots were of no value to the Philistines.

Ramathaim-Zophim, *Ramah of the Watchers*, comprised two hills with watchtowers. And while their high position gave the city a view of the surrounding plains, the forests covering the hills were a perfect hiding spot for enemy soldiers bent on conquering their village. Elkanah had spoken of the idol worship that had crept into the practices of their people, a symptom of the uncertainty and fear that seemed to hang in the air like a heavy fog. It was happening in their village just as it was throughout all the tribes of Israel, an uneasy merging of tradition and desperation.

As Hannah and Ayala entered the village, the distant calls of vendors and the clatter of carts were muffled as if the air held its breath, waiting. Hannah tasted the worry in the dry wind rustling through the olive trees. The hardened dirt road beneath her feet seemed more uneven than usual and mirrored the turmoil in her heart.

Leading Ayala through the streets toward their home near the wide-open fields, Hannah couldn't help but stare at her neighbors as they hurried home earlier in the day than usual. Their faces, once familiar and friendly, held shadows of unease. Worried gazes met hers.

The village had changed. Fear overshadowed the simple joys of home and family. Yet instead of seeking only Yahweh, many in the village had turned to the Canaanite gods.

Baal, the Canaanite god of weather, was believed by some to have control over the fertility of crops, animals, and people. His appeal had grown amongst the farmers and herdsmen of the village who were desperate for prosperous seasons.

Asherah, the so-called goddess of the sea and wife of El, had found many followers too. The people who worshiped all three clung to the empty promise of a balance of land and water, growth and sustenance.

Chemosh was another idol gaining attention. The unease caused by the threat of enemy soldiers hiding in the nearby forests drove some villagers to seek favor of this savage war god, hoping for victory and safety through his brutal might.

The idol worship was evidence of the villagers' fear and confusion. Once united under their faith in Yahweh, the village was now fracturing, with pockets of people seeking different deities, each promising relief.

The traditions of Hannah's people, and her faith in Yahweh, were being challenged by the desperation she saw. Her neighbors' faces, which once reflected shared beliefs, now revealed doubt, fear, and a willingness to seek answers from the Canaanite gods.

Ayala must have sensed Hannah's thoughts, adding to the girl's own worry. Ayala tugged at her hand. "Will everything be all right?"

"Yes, dear one. Everything will be fine."

But as they reached their dwelling and the door closed behind them, Hannah hoped she had told the truth.

They had just removed their sandals when the door burst open. Peninnah swept into the main living area. She carried her youngest son, Zemir, on her hip, with her other sons trailing behind. The family servants bustled in after her, arms laden with market goods.

Hannah stepped out of their way, moving toward a long serving table—Ayala's hand still in hers. There was something in Peninnah's eyes, a gleam of triumph, that sent a shiver down Hannah's spine.

"Ah, Hannah," Peninnah called, her voice lilting, "I have wonderful news. The Lord has blessed me once again. I am with child."

The room seemed to spin, Peninnah's words like a knife to Hannah's heart. She staggered, and Ayala's confused face looked up at her.

The scent of the fresh produce brought in by the servants turned sour in Hannah's nostrils. The bright colors of the fruits and vegetables blurred in her vision.

The boys' laughter as they rushed up to Ayala contrasted with the agony that twisted within Hannah. They urged Ayala to play with them in the courtyard, but Ayala clung tighter to Hannah's hand. The boys ran out the back door, and Hannah considered calling and telling them to stay inside. They needed to remain together, to stay safe, in case their enemy arrived, but the words stuck in Hannah's throat.

The room seemed to tilt. Hannah released Ayala's hand and reached forward to steady herself. The feel of the rough wooden table beneath her fingertips was the only thing grounding her and keeping her from collapsing. Even the threat of an enemy soldier or the attack of the Philistines could not have wounded her so deeply.

She looked closer at Peninnah. The younger woman's face glowed. The gentle curve of pregnancy was evident even with the toddler's legs wrapped around his mother's waist. The way Peninnah held herself, the smug satisfaction in her expression was a torment Hannah could hardly bear.

The room was bursting with the sounds of life, the chatter of servants, the clatter of pots. But all Hannah could hear was the echoing emptiness within her soul.

"Hannah?" Peninnah's voice was softer now, and Hannah knew she feigned concern. Why she bothered to do so was a mystery. The servants knew of her disdain for Hannah. "Are you well? You look so pale."

"I—I am fine," Hannah stammered, forcing a smile. Tears burned behind her eyes. "Congratulations, Peninnah."

But the words were bitter ashes in her mouth. Hannah turned away, unable to bear Peninnah's silent mockery, her mind a whirl of pain and doubt.

Did the Lord truly hear her prayers? Was her barrenness a punishment, a sign of His displeasure? Was she destined to forever live in Peninnah's shadow?

Only Ayala's cries broke through the darkness swirling in Hannah's clouded thoughts.

Ayala stared at her mother in what looked like disbelief… and sadness. "Another baby?" The little girl sank to the floor.

Barely giving her daughter a side glance, Peninnah heaved a sigh. Then she strode to the side of the house that contained her sleeping quarters. She mumbled something about changing the baby, but Hannah knew it was an excuse. Ayala did too. Peninnah didn't seem to know how to handle her daughter's disappointment, and she didn't make an effort to try.

Hannah pressed a hand to her forehead, hoping to keep the ache away. This was not good news for Ayala either.

The little girl's eyes locked with Hannah's. They were both overlooked and ignored. But as Hannah considered what words of comfort she could offer the girl, a trumpet blasted. A chill ran down Hannah's spine. Were the Philistines attacking? And what about Elkanah? He would be among the first to join the other men to protect their town and families.

As the trumpet blew a second time, Hannah's cheeks heated. She should be ashamed, crying about her unmet desire when a real enemy was at their gates. Even though she had grown weary of praying, wondering if her prayers were even heard, she sank to her knees and invited Ayala to join her. Elkanah needed their prayers. All the men of the village did.

CHAPTER TWO

Ten Years Later

A decade had etched its imprint on Hannah's soul, yet she could clearly remember the day when she pushed aside her prayers for a child and locked them away. The Philistines had attacked all those years ago, and Hannah couldn't forget how bravely Elkanah fought. Even though he was more skilled with a lyre than a bow, her husband had rallied the other men and led them to protect their village. They held the enemy at bay, but two young men were killed in the attack near the creek where she had sat praying. If her husband had not come, she might have been one of the victims. Besides, what had her prayers mattered? If Yahweh saw fit to give her a child, He would. She would hope, but her prayers hadn't done any good.

Now the sounds of fighting rose again, from Elkanah's sons scrimmaging in the courtyard behind their home. Hannah washed the leeks and garlic and watched the boisterous spectacle through the open doorway as the gangly young men battled with wooden swords. She grimaced as the fake weapons clashed with exhilarating thuds.

"Ha! Take that, Philistine scum!" one of the boys yelled, thrusting his sword at his brother, who played the part of the enemy.

"Oh, I am so scared!" the other brother mocked, dodging the strike with a laugh. "You will have to do better than that to defeat a mighty Philistine warrior!"

After mincing the vegetables, Hannah retrieved a handful of dried lentils from the last harvest. She rinsed the tiny flat disks in a bowl of water, the cool liquid running through her fingers, washing away the dust and chaff.

The family's cookstove was a mud-brick construction, fired with wood that the younger boys gathered. Hannah stoked the flames, watching them dance. She placed a well-worn clay pot over the heat. Into the pot went a splash of oil, followed by the chopped leeks and garlic, their aroma filling the air as they sizzled and softened. Next she added the lentils, water, herbs, and a pinch of salt.

The lentils simmered. She occasionally stirred them with a wooden spoon, still watching the boys' spirited game unfold in the courtyard. Their laughter mingled with the savory scents of the simmering meal and the fresh bread baked by the servants that morning. A bittersweet smile tugged at the corners of Hannah's mouth as her eyes followed their agile movements.

The boys lunged and parried, their faces lit with fierce determination. Pausing her task, Hannah moved to get a better view.

The boys' tunics reached their knees, secured with a belt around each waist. Their hair was dark and untrimmed, cascading down their shoulders and curling at the ends. Elkanah's features were evident in the eldest boys' faces, with their strong jawlines and expressive eyes. Their bodies moved with natural grace, like their father. But Hannah could also see the features of Peninnah. Peninnah's lively and vibrant children were a constant reminder of Hannah's empty arms.

Elkanah raised his sons with the values and customs of their faith and community. Obedience to their parents, respect for the elders, and understanding their role in their family's survival were ingrained in them. Even their games, such as their mock battle with the Philistines, were influenced by the stories and teachings they heard from their abba and elders.

As Hannah watched the boys, her mind wandered in want of the son she still desperately wished for. Would he have his abba's soulful eyes? Or the musical talents of the Levites? She could almost hear his laughter mingling with that of his half brothers. Could almost imagine him sparring outside with the others.

Beyond the boys lay the fields. All around them, the land was coming to life with the promise of spring.

Barley fields swayed gently in the breeze—tender green stalks reaching for the sky. It would not be long before they would turn golden and be ready for harvest. Elkanah's family would soon make their pilgrimage to Shiloh for the Feast of Unleavened Bread, a time of remembrance and reflection on Yahweh's deliverance from the land of Egypt. Olive trees budded, silvery leaves glinting in the sunlight. Grapevines bloomed, hinting at the abundance of wine to come. The air carried the songs of birds returning from their winter migration, and the fragrance of almond blossoms and fresh earth drifted in the open doorway and windows, filling Hannah's senses as she anticipated the sacred journey and the solemn yet joyous observance of the feast in Shiloh.

Sheep grazed contentedly on the lush grass, tended by faithful servants who were ever watchful for predators or stray lambs. The scene was idyllic, a portrait of Yahweh's provision and the blessings of the land. She had so much to be thankful for, yet a deep yearning dulled her soul to all these things.

A pang of longing tugged at her heart like the insistent pull of a plow on hardened soil. Nearly two decades of wishing for a son weighed heavily on her soul. The joy of spring, the renewal of life, and the preparations for Passover only accentuated her emptiness, like a fallow field awaiting seed.

More than anything, Hannah wished she still clung to her faith, drawing strength from the traditions and rituals that had sustained her people for generations. For many years she had. *But now?*

Elkanah was soon to choose the Passover lamb, its pure blood a poignant symbol of deliverance and redemption. It would be a tangible reminder that those who were once enslaved were now free. But what did freedom truly mean? Was it an endless worry over the constant looming threats of the Philistines? Or the disgruntled mumblings of citizens who longed to be like other nations—with a king to lead them into battle?

Then there were the rumors concerning Eli's sons. The high priest, revered and respected for his dedication to Yahweh, seemed to disregard the transgressions of his sons, his own flesh and blood. This willful ignorance did not feel like freedom to Hannah.

Neither did the dark cloud that perpetually hovered over her. No matter how much sunshine bathed her face or how sweet the birdsong sounded or how enticing the fragrant aromas of the countryside were, a hollow echo rang louder within her. A constant, gnawing emptiness. No matter the gifts the land bestowed, the support of the servants, or even the love and attention her husband showered upon her, everything placed in Hannah's hands seemed to bear the cruel mark of "not enough."

Worse still, this mark etched a permanent tattoo onto Hannah's soul. The lamb's blood might symbolize redemption, but it could not wash away the painful sense of insufficiency that defined her existence. Hannah believed in a Yahweh who had seen the tears of His people in Egypt and led them to freedom. Yet she still wasn't sure if Yahweh knew her or cared about her.

Turning back to her work inside the house, Hannah was startled to find Elkanah standing inside the kitchen watching her, his gaze thoughtful and probing.

"You find their antics amusing?" he asked, his voice gentle.

Hannah's smile faltered, and she looked away. "Yes, they are quite the performers. It is good to see them so engaged."

An awkward silence followed. Elkanah's eyes searched her face. Did he see the ache in her soul?

Hannah broke the silence. "Why are you home during the day? Is there news of another Philistine attack?"

Elkanah shook his head, relief softening his features. "No, there is no news of an attack. I came home early because I knew

Peninnah was gone for the day. She is visiting Ayala to see how my daughter is setting up her new home."

My *daughter, instead of* our *daughter.* The phrasing did not escape her notice.

Hannah sighed, still finding it hard to believe that the young woman who used to trail her as a little girl was now married. Even harder to believe was the gentle tenderness in her own husband's gaze. They had spent the first three years of their marriage together without distraction, but once Peninnah joined as a second wife and children rapidly joined the family, time alone with Elkanah was rare.

"You knew Peninnah would be gone, so you came home to spend time with me?" Hannah pushed the small pile of leftover leeks to the side and wiped her hands on the apron around her waist. Her heart quickened as if she were again a young bride like Ayala. Yet she pressed her lips tightly. No, she was no longer a young bride with hopes and dreams. Reality had stripped her of both.

Elkanah chuckled, a warm sound that resonated with years of shared memories and love. Once bright with youthful exuberance, his eyes now held a depth of wisdom and perhaps a touch of weariness. The lines on his face spoke of decades of joy, sorrow, and responsibility.

"When I first saw you, you were like a refreshing spring on a parched day," he said, his voice tender with reminiscence. "I was drawn to you, not only by your beauty but by the purity of your devotion to Yahweh."

Hannah's heart swelled at his words, but she could not ignore the changes time had wrought. The young man she had fallen in love with, so full of vigor and passion, had matured into a man bearing the weight of his duties as a Levite. The fire was still there, but now it was tempered by experience and burdened with their community's cares—and his growing family.

Elkanah's face was etched with worry and sadness, reflecting his anguish over his people's waywardness. "I long for our people to have that same devotion." He sighed. "I see them bowing before statues and images, Hannah," he confessed, his voice breaking. "They seek solace in these false gods, forgetting the covenant we made with Yahweh. It is as though the teachings of Moses and the wisdom of our forefathers have been cast aside."

Over the last decade, the faith of the Hebrews had continued to splinter. Their once-unified devotion to Yahweh became more fragmented with each passing year, seduced by the allure of false idols. The whispers of apostasy were growing louder, and many of Elkanah's kinsmen fell prey to the tempting promises of foreign gods. They constructed altars to Baal and Asherah, turning their backs on the Yahweh of their ancestors.

Hannah watched Elkanah, noting how his gaze swept over their bustling village, no doubt noting the decreasing numbers of families immersed in preparations for the impending pilgrimage. Though filled with the joyful shrieks of children and the rhythmic noises of carts being loaded and animals being herded, the air also held a note of sadness and an echo of former vibrancy.

Underneath the surface-level excitement, a shadow lurked. The eagerness on many faces was a facade, hiding an emptiness born from abandoned faith.

"How can I lead them when their spirits are so adrift?" he whispered.

Her husband was enmeshed in a quiet battle, a lonely endeavor to lead the lost out of the shadows and back into Yahweh's embrace. She knew that every step he took toward Shiloh, every prayer he uttered in hushed tones in the sanctuary included a silent hope for their kinsfolk's spiritual awakening and salvation. Fewer and fewer chose to even go on the pilgrimage. And she suspected that even those who prepared were driven by the remnants of tradition rather than a genuine desire to worship Yahweh.

Hannah touched his cheek, her eyes full of understanding and love. "You lead with your faith, Elkanah. You guide them with your devotion to Yahweh and unwavering belief in His laws. We may not be able to change the people's hearts, but we can live our lives by His commandments."

A smile touched Elkanah's lips. She hoped the warmth of her encouragement helped ease his troubled soul. "I am blessed to have you by my side," he whispered, embracing her tightly.

Their relationship had also evolved from the fiery romance of youth to a more complex love, weathered by trials. But alongside the sweet memories was the shadow of unfulfilled longing.

Elkanah seemed to sense her thoughts. He reached for her hand and squeezed it gently. "We have each other and Yahweh's love. That is enough. For today at least."

But was it? Hannah's eyes filled with tears, and she looked away as a bitter taste filled her mouth. Even in this tender moment, the emptiness echoed, a constant reminder of what they lacked.

Elkanah leaned forward. "And choosing you was the smartest decision I have ever made, although convincing your abba that a Levite musician was good enough for his daughter was a challenge."

Hannah's heart skipped a beat at his words. Yet was there something more in his eyes? Something he wasn't saying? It had to be more than fond memories that drew him home early.

"It will be a different journey this year, won't it?" She tucked a strand of hair behind her ear. "With the boys getting older. And even little Leeba won't have to be carried as often. Only one baby to be passed around to be carried." *Peninnah's last one*, she dared to speculate. After Ayala and the five boys, many years went by before Leeba joined them three years prior and Tobiah last year.

Elkanah nodded, his expression showing an understanding that reached beyond words. "Yes, but maybe next year things will be even more different." His hand tightened around hers, his grip firm yet gentle, as he pulled her hand to his chest, guiding her to step closer.

With a delicate release of her fingers, Hannah responded by splaying them across his chest, over his heart. The rough fabric of his tunic, warmed by the sun, felt reassuring against her palm, and the steady beat of his heart helped to soothe her restless soul.

"I have not given up hope," he whispered, his voice carrying a conviction that challenged her despair.

Hannah's eyes widened, and she tilted her head, a fragile spark igniting. "Hope?"

"Yes, my wife. Hope. For us. For a child." His voice wavered slightly, and he struggled to contain the emotion in his words. "Have you?"

Her gaze met his, and she saw the reflection of her longing and uncertainty in his eyes. It was a question she had asked herself many thousands of times, a battle she fought within her soul every day.

Elkanah's dark eyes fixed on hers, so intense she had to look away. Then the uneasiness between them deepened, and she pulled away from him and busied herself with her work, trying to shake off the nagging feeling that he wanted her to spout a faith she did not feel. Did her husband wonder if she still pleaded with Yahweh? And what would he think if she didn't?

Elkanah continued to watch her, his presence a silent question. The sounds of the boys' laughter and the clash of swords drifted in from outside again, contrasting the quiet tension in the air.

Finally, Hannah knew she could not ignore Elkanah any longer. She dared to look back over her shoulder. "Do *you* pray still for this?" She felt her forehead folding in question. She didn't have to explain. They both knew her meaning. *Do you still pray for him? A son? Our son?*

"I have not stopped praying for a child for us. And lately..." Elkanah's voice trailed off.

A child for us. The pain struck Hannah's heart, slicing like a knife blade. Pressing a trembling hand to her lips, she held her husband's gaze. Tears threatened. Could she pray?

Her husband's penetrating gaze told her he wanted to say more. But did she want to hear it?

Hannah couldn't make a promise to pray. Not today, at least. Yet her heart softened as she peered into her husband's kind face. "I am looking forward to going to Shiloh. There is nothing like joining with others in song. In praise." Her words rushed out, partly because she didn't want to speak any more of their mutual longing. After so many years, what good would come of it? And hadn't she just wondered if Peninnah's childbearing years were past? Hannah was older than her husband's second wife.

Hannah's thoughts drifted again to the first time she and Elkanah met. That year, Rina, the choir director, had asked her to join the choir for the Passover celebration at Shiloh. It was a rare honor.

The Passover was a time of great rejoicing—a festival that commemorated the Israelites' deliverance from slavery in Egypt. Choirs joined in praising Yahweh and leading the people in song during the celebration. She had felt her heart swell with pride and devotion as she joined in the songs of praise.

But more than the honor, that year was special because of Elkanah. He, a young Levite, watched her, with both admiration and something more profound. The connection was instant.

"I remember," Elkanah said softly, his voice tinged with nostalgia. "Your voice was like a clear, sweet melody, a song that spoke directly to my heart."

Hannah smiled, her eyes misting with the memory. "And I remember you, standing there, so earnest, so full of faith. It was as if Yahweh Himself determined our paths would cross."

The memories of that first Passover celebration flooded back, and she could almost feel the lightness that had filled her heart as she joined with others in song. The unity of voices, the sense of purpose, and the connection to something greater than themselves made her feel alive and joyful.

Is it possible to feel even a glimmer of that again? Hannah wondered, a longing deep in her soul. Had her heart shriveled beyond recognition? Or was there still a spark there, waiting to be rekindled?

"I remember the song we were singing at that moment," she said, her voice soft but emotional. "The one about Yahweh's faithfulness, the one we sang as we prepared for the feast. 'Yahweh's love endures forever, His mercy knows no end, He led us from the land of bondage, Our Yahweh, our Savior, our friend.'"

As the words left her lips, she saw a brightness on Elkanah's face. The light mirrored her feelings, and her heart stirred. Impulsively, wanting to capture a bit of what they had both lost, she said, "Do you think they will let me join this year? Be part of the choir of singers? Is it too late to ask?"

Elkanah rocked on his feet and clapped his hands. There was a spiritedness to his movements that she hadn't seen in so long. "I will talk to the others. We will go to Shiloh with a new song on our lips this year."

Hannah's heart swelled at her husband's enthusiasm.

He stepped forward and wrapped his hands around Hannah's upper arms, his touch gentle but urgent. At that moment, with thoughts of being part of the choir again—and seeing her husband's joy—the burdens of the previous years lifted. Laughter rose and slipped from Hannah's mouth.

Elkanah released her arms, captured her hands, and pulled them to his chest, his eyes shining. "Yes." His voice was strong with conviction. "Let us reclaim that joy. Let us go to Shiloh with new hope, a renewed spirit, and a song in our hearts. Yahweh has been faithful in bringing us together, and He will be faithful—"

Hannah rose on her toes, cutting off her husband's words with a kiss. Pulling back, he looked down with a surprised smile.

Something stirred deep within her. A passion reignited? A renewed hope? Hannah found herself drawn toward Elkanah, leaning closer, her heart pounding. But just as she stood on her toes to offer another kiss, the front door creaked open wide, startling them both.

Hannah jumped away, her face flushed with embarrassment at being caught. Then the frustration of being unable to share even a simple kiss with her husband surged—a hot and irritating emotion that made her feel trapped and invaded.

An intimate, beautiful moment between husband and wife ripped away so abruptly, as it often was by Peninnah's moods.

Hannah was left with a heavy feeling of loss, knowing that Peninnah's presence had once again cast a shadow over her relationship with Elkanah.

Peninnah's eyes flared with anger as she looked first at Hannah and then at Elkanah. Her face twisted into a scowl directed at her husband. "What are you doing here?"

CHAPTER THREE

E lkanah released his tender grasp of Hannah's hands, and his eyes hardened. "It is my home," he stated. He offered no other explanation, and Peninnah demanded no other answer. How could she? Still, she did not move.

The room seemed to grow colder. The gentle warmth of moments ago was gone, replaced by a suffocating heaviness. Hannah's hands dropped from Elkanah's chest, and she stepped back. Her eyes locked with Peninnah's. An unspoken challenge flared in Peninnah's stare.

Even after all these years, Peninnah still saw Hannah as a threat. Hannah would not stoop to her level. She knew she had Elkanah's heart, though marriages were not always built on love.

Hannah moved to stir the lentils, trying to lose herself in the simple task. But the growing unease was impossible to ignore. Elkanah too remained quiet. Looking back at him, Hannah noted her husband now looked haggard. In his face, she saw the same weariness that had settled in her own heart, the strain of navigating Peninnah's moods, and the heavy weight of his responsibilities to his family and the Levites. She understood why he would remain quiet, choosing his battles carefully, avoiding unnecessary conflict. She often did the same, though more than once she questioned why.

"I do not understand why we do not have more packed for the journey." Peninnah's voice was edged with annoyance. Her eyes flashed with anger as she fixed them on her husband. "We have to leave in two days, do we not?" Her question sounded more like an accusation, as if every detail concerning their journey rested on Peninnah's shoulders.

Peninnah was still a beauty. Her black hair, rich as midnight, framed a face that radiated charm and delight, at least upon first meeting. Her eyes, dark and sparkling, had a way of captivating anyone she spoke to, making them feel as if they were the only person in the room. When she chose to share it, her smile could light up a space, and her laughter was infectious.

Yet behind the attractive exterior lay a vengeful and cunning character. It was a character that had revealed itself slowly to Hannah, showing glimpses only when Peninnah's guard was down or when she felt particularly bold.

Hannah understood why Elkanah had taken a second wife. It was not uncommon, especially if the first wife bore no children. A practical solution to a heartbreaking problem, ensuring the continuation of the family line.

Hannah had never asked him why he chose Peninnah, and she only met her after the marriage had already occurred. On that first meeting, Peninnah said all the right things. Many times since, Hannah wondered if not meeting her sooner had been a mistake. Would she have discovered Peninnah's true character? Might Hannah have had a chance to warn her husband? Yet even if she had, would he have listened?

On Hannah's best days, she pitied the younger woman. The sixth daughter in a line of daughters, all even more beautiful than she. And then to marry someone who already had a wife he loved. Like Leah, their ancestor, at least Peninnah could give her husband many children. Unlike Leah and Rachel, Peninnah had no fondness or previous relationship with Hannah that would make her care for Hannah even a little bit. Her beauty and ability to bear children became her triumph. And Hannah's curse.

Elkanah's gaze met Peninnah's. "Our family has made this pilgrimage many times, and we always manage."

Yet even as he spoke, Elkanah briefly looked to Hannah in a quick apology. Was he apologizing for Peninnah's behavior, or his own in not reprimanding her? Hannah wasn't sure.

"We have time yet, Peninnah," Hannah added, her voice even and calm. "Everything will be prepared for our journey to Shiloh. You need not worry so."

Peninnah bristled. Her sense of betrayal, albeit unfounded, was written all over her face. Moods like this often took days, if not weeks, to settle. Preparing for the trip to Shiloh, with all the people, tents, food, and articles needed for Elkanah's Levitical tasks, was enough work. Contending with Peninnah's moods added unnecessary weight to their already heavy burden. The unease in the room lingered, a subtle yet palpable foreshadowing of the tension that would likely accompany them on the journey ahead.

Peninnah turned to Hannah, her voice lowering but still taut with tension. "Hannah, have you packed clean tunics for your sons? Have you baked bread for their meals?" The younger wife scoffed with disdain.

The words stung, and heat rose to Hannah's cheeks, a burning blend of embarrassment and anger. It was a pointed reminder of her childlessness, a wound that Peninnah enjoyed poking. Hannah's hands clenched, but she kept her voice steady. "Everything will be ready in time," she said, refusing to let Peninnah see how deeply her words cut.

Tension in the room remained thick and palpable, like a cloud that threatened to burst into a storm. Hannah suspected that Peninnah's worries about the preparations for the journey to Shiloh were a facade. Did Peninnah guess that Elkanah had come home early, knowing she would be away?

Blowing out a breath, Peninnah strode to Elkanah's side. "Ayala is feeling under the weather. Knowing I was coming, she sent one of her servants to meet me. That was thoughtful, don't you think?"

"Yes, quite thoughtful indeed," Elkanah answered. "Hannah, would you make me some tea, please? And later we will say a prayer for Ayala's health."

Hannah quickly moved to do as her husband asked, grateful for the task. She filled a pot with water and placed it over the open flames. With hands that had performed the ritual countless times, she reached for the dried herbs and spices stored in earthen jars. She carefully selected a blend that might diffuse the tension in the room. The scent of mint, anise, and chamomile filled the air as she crushed the desiccated leaves with a mortar and pestle.

Once the water came to a gentle boil, she added the crushed herbs, allowing them to steep, then poured the tea into clay mugs. The steam rose in gentle spirals.

She handed a cup to Elkanah first. Elkanah's eyes met hers, gratitude shining as he accepted the cup. She handed another to Peninnah, who accepted it but did not meet Hannah's gaze. Hannah knew that the truce would be temporary. Peninnah's barbs had found their mark, and the younger woman would exult in her perceived victory.

Hannah sipped her own tea and noticed the older boys had put down their wooden swords and were now helping their younger brothers stack the collected wood near the open doorway. The oldest son, Eitan, peered in. He was clearly surprised to see his father home early. But then his expression changed, as though he sensed the icy chill in the air. With a shrug, Eitan motioned his brothers toward the small enclosure they had built for the Passover lambs, using the excuse of refreshing their water.

Her husband released a sigh. Did Peninnah's words bother him? Or were they a sharp reminder of the reality of the situation? He finished his tea and set the cup at his place at the table.

Hannah checked the lentils. Already they were transforming from their hardened state to a tender, flavorful stew. How she wished her hardened heart could be so easily softened. Once a comforting routine, the cooking of this nourishing meal now mocked her. This food, so lovingly prepared, was to feed Peninnah's children.

She moved the pot from the flame and covered it, trapping the warmth and allowing the lentils to finish cooking off the heat. The meal was nearly ready.

Elkanah cleared his throat. His voice, when he finally spoke to Peninnah, was even yet determined. "We will be ready. We must be."

"Yes, we must be, Husband." Peninnah edged closer, and her stern gaze turned into a wide-eyed glance, toning down her harshness as she often did when Elkanah was present. "You have special duties we cannot forget." The younger wife inched closer and attempted a compassionate look that didn't quite seem sincere.

Even though Elkanah was a Levite, he lived far from the central sanctuary in Shiloh. The Tribe of Levi had no contiguous parcel of land. Instead, she knew that the Levites were assigned to dwell in certain cities scattered throughout the tribes of Israel. And like all Levites, Elkanah's family's responsibilities varied yearly. Levitical service was organized so that various Levite families rotated duties for three festivals, including Passover. In some years, Elkanah's role was extensive, overseeing sacrifices, guiding the rituals, and ensuring the laws were meticulously followed.

This year was one of those when the burden of responsibility lay heavy on Elkanah's shoulders. He was to assist in choosing the unblemished lambs, preparing the ritual meals, and teaching the meaning of the festival to the community's younger generations. It was a time to remember how the Lord had delivered their people from Egypt's bondage and a reminder that obedience to Yahweh's law was paramount.

Hannah listened to the exchange between Elkanah and Peninnah as they discussed the new garments recently sewn to fit their growing sons. As she put away the herbs for the tea, her mind drifted to tomorrow's preparations. She would be busy grinding grain for the unleavened bread, gathering bitter herbs, and cleaning the house to ensure no trace of leaven remained. Though the tasks were always performed with love and dedication in preparation for the upcoming festival, over the years they had lost some of their meaning in the shadow of her longing for a child, a dream, it seemed, that was never to be fulfilled.

Elkanah reminded Peninnah to pack Eitan's new robes. His oldest son would stand beside him for the first time as he performed the rituals that had defined their people for generations.

Elkanah's face reflected the gravity of his duties and his spiritual legacy as he spoke. He was a Levite of the family of Kohath, the son of Jeroham, the son of Elihu, who was the son of Tohu and Zuph. He was a watcher of the tabernacle, an overseer of the sacred rituals, and a keeper of the laws handed down by Moses. His position was one of honor and responsibility, and he bore it with a weight that Hannah could see, even as she felt disconnected from its purpose.

Hannah moved to sit beside her husband, a moment's rest before telling him that dinner was ready. Every day Elkanah taught his sons about Yahweh's ordinances and their responsibilities as Levites. He desired his boys to respect his words and teaching, which meant wearing clean garments, observing the ritual cleanliness, and preparing for their roles as future leaders in the religious community.

Elkanah reached over and took her hand under the table, a small gesture of connection that warmed her heart.

"Of course, you could not understand, Hannah," Peninnah purred, her eyes glinting maliciously. "It is very trying to pack for so many family members. Maybe not having a child is not such a curse, not on days like today when the tasks that need to be completed appear to have no end, yes?" The words slipped off her tongue with a hiss.

"Peninnah," Elkanah admonished, "we all have our burdens to bear. We will not trivialize the pain of others. We must support each other as a family should." His grip on Hannah's hand tightened, a silent bastion of reassurance amid the tempest of words.

Though Hannah saw the anger and betrayal in Peninnah's eyes, she remained silent.

"Hannah." Elkanah's voice was gentle.

The darkness bore down.

"Hannah," he repeated.

She dared to look up. She saw the mirror of her pain mixed with determination in his face. It both frightened and fortified her. Yet just as determined was Peninnah's gaze upon them both. And Hannah knew that if she dared to cling to any thread of hope, Peninnah would do her best to strip it away.

Elkanah put his lips to Hannah's ear. "I will speak to the choir director," he whispered. "They need your voice. But more than that, you need Yahweh's song."

Hannah's lips quivered, and she nodded, her eyes briefly meeting Peninnah's. The woman was barely containing her anger, likely from being excluded from Elkanah's private conversation. Living with Peninnah was like navigating a field full of hidden snares, never knowing when the next trap might spring. The echoes of hidden dangers accompanied her every step, her daily life a precarious balance.

"I need to gather some herbs," Hannah murmured, her voice barely above a whisper, her heart pounding like the hooves of wild donkeys fleeing across the rugged Judean landscape. "That stew needs a bit more flavor." And suddenly she needed some time to herself.

Elkanah nodded. Concern shadowed his eyes, but he said nothing to her. Instead, he turned to Peninnah. "Go ask some servants to help you prepare the children for dinner. The food smells wonderful, and we should not delay."

As Hannah moved to retrieve her scarf and basket, she could feel Peninnah's scrutiny like a physical touch. Without a look over her shoulder, Hannah hurried away, her feet carrying her down the path along the barley field to the wilder parts of their land, the coarse dirt crunching beneath her sandals.

She knew gathering the herbs wouldn't take long, but she needed a moment away from Peninnah. As she passed one of the outbuildings, she encountered one of the servants,

Shifrah, a woman hard at work grinding grain with a stone mill, her hands covered with flour. The rhythmic grinding provided a calming backdrop to Hannah's thoughts.

"Going to find herbs, Mistress Hannah?" the servant asked, noting the basket, her eyes twinkling with a knowing look.

"Yes," Hannah replied, her voice soft but warm. "The *maror* for Passover."

The servant chuckled, brushing a strand of hair from her forehead with her flour-dusted hand. "Ah, the bitter herbs. A fine ingredient for any dish, but some might say we have enough bitterness around here without adding more."

Hannah's eyes widened briefly before she realized that the jest was a playful reference to Peninnah's sharp tongue. A smile tugged at the corner of her mouth.

"I suppose you are right," she said. "But we must honor tradition, mustn't we?"

"Indeed we must." The servant's eyes sparkled with mirth. "But sometimes, a sprinkle of sweetness can balance the bitterness quite nicely."

They both laughed, a shared understanding passing between them, a momentary connection that eased the burden on Hannah's heart.

"Thank you," Hannah said softly.

"May Yahweh bless your gathering," Shifrah responded sincerely.

Behind her, Hannah heard Elkanah summoning the boys. "Enough playing, my sons! The lambs are thirsty, and it is time for dinner and evening prayers."

She paused and turned to see obedient yet reluctant boys, one of them picking up the waiting bucket of water.

They poured the cool water into the trough for the year-old lambs, who ran eagerly toward the refreshing liquid, their bleats filling the air.

Everyone was acutely aware of why these particular lambs were being set apart. These innocent creatures, symbols of purity and sacrifice, were destined for a higher purpose, reflecting the sacred and the divine in their simple existence.

As she continued along the path, the servant's words about sweetness lingered in Hannah's mind, sparking a realization. It struck her that she was missing Ayala, Peninnah's daughter. And she was also a bit concerned. Peninnah had said that Ayala was not feeling well.

Ayala's disposition was the opposite of her mother's. Even during hard days, Hannah looked forward to conversations with the girl, now a young woman. Ayala's cheerful nature and gentle spirit had always brightened their home.

She smiled as she thought about how Ayala and her new husband would join their journey to Shiloh. That was some-thing Hannah could look forward to—a sweet respite amid the complex emotions the upcoming festival brought.

Then an idea blossomed in her mind. Peninnah was right. Hannah had fewer responsibilities for the preparation of the journey. She would have time to visit Ayala in the morning. Surely Elkanah would appreciate her going to check on her and help the young woman pack for her first trip to Shiloh as a wife. A shared moment of joy and anticipation before the journey could be the sprinkle of sweetness she needed to balance the bitterness in her heart and in her home.

With renewed purpose, Hannah quickened her pace. After dinner, she would share her plans with Elkanah. The path to Shiloh was beginning to reveal itself, and Hannah was starting to see a glimmer of its promise.

CHAPTER FOUR

T he sun dipped below the horizon, casting a golden glow over the fields surrounding Hannah's home. The barley swayed gently in the breeze, rippling like a sea of green and gold. From her vantage point, she could see the ancient tower standing sentinel on the edge of their property. Its solid stone structure, weathered by the years, was a constant presence, a watchful eye over their land.

Even though she could not see him, she knew one of their young servants sat at the top of the tower with his waterskin and a loaf of barley bread, scanning the countryside below the hills, ever vigilant against Philistine invaders. Except for a few stray bands of rogues, no severe threat had come during the past year, but that didn't mean anything. The Philistines knew the Hebrew calendar just as well as her people did. She wouldn't put it past them to attack during a time when the villagers would be packing for their spiritual pilgrimage to Shiloh.

Hannah's hands trembled as she plucked the sharp-leaved plants—each stem she snapped was a tangible reminder of her ache. The scent of the maror was tangy and biting. Finally, with a basket full of the bitter herbs, Hannah rose, her knees aching.

She returned home just in time to quickly wash for the evening meal. As Peninnah settled the youngest children on the bench next to her, Hannah lifted the gently bubbling stew and carried it toward the outside table.

Their home was modest but lovingly cared for, with earthen walls and a thatched roof. The courtyard, where the family gathered for meals and prayers, was enclosed by a low stone wall and dotted with olive and fig trees. In the early years of Hannah's marriage, it had been a sanctuary where faith and family converged and hope in Yahweh's care was as tangible as the cool evening breeze.

They gathered around the wooden table, sitting on low cushions. Before them lay the pot of lentil stew and a plate of barley bread. As the family settled for the meal, Hannah began serving them, her hands moving with practiced ease. Peninnah sat in stony silence. Even though she found ways to mock or berate Hannah during the day—even in front of Elkanah— she didn't often do so in front of her children.

One of the younger boys, eyes wide with anticipation, turned to Elkanah. "Abba, will we see the great altar in Shiloh again? The one with the horns where the offerings are burned?"

"Yes, my son." Elkanah smiled at his child's curiosity. "And we will join in the prayers and songs, just as we have in years past."

One of the older boys chimed in, a grin spreading across his face, "And do not forget the food during the feast, little brother! It is as if the entire land of Canaan gathers to eat and celebrate together."

The boys' joy and vitality were infectious, and Hannah's shoulders relaxed. After she served each person, she took her place beside Elkanah.

Elkanah led the family in a brief prayer of gratitude before breaking the bread and passing it along. Hannah took a piece, feeling the coarse texture in her hands. She dipped it into the lentil stew then took a bite. The earthy taste of the lentils blended perfectly with the nutty flavor of the barley bread.

The sounds of the family enjoying their meal filled the air. The gentle slurping of the stew, the contented sighs. As the sky darkened, the flickering light from an oil lamp brought by a servant cast a warm glow over the faces of those she loved. And those she tried to love.

Then, from the end of the table, a soft fussing caught her attention. Tobiah was squirming in his chair, a cry threatening to erupt. The instinct to soothe the baby tugged at Hannah, but she left him to his mother and turned to Ya'akov instead. "Tell me, my dear, do you think the lentils are as good as last time?"

The little boy shrugged in answer and took another large bite of bread.

"And are you excited about our journey in a few days?" she asked.

This time he responded with an enthusiastic nod.

As the conversation around her turned to the upcoming celebrations, Hannah's mind wandered back to her childhood, to the times of celebration when her family would journey to the sacred place. Even as a child, she had looked forward to the annual feast and the bond she felt with others there, connected by their history, their faith, and the mighty hand of Yahweh.

No matter what one did or did not have at home, everyone celebrated together. Rich or poor, master or servant, young or old, everyone gathered to remember and give thanks.

Her eyes flickered toward Elkanah, and her heart swelled with love for this good man, who not only upheld these sacred traditions but instilled them in his children.

"But it is not just about the food, is it, Abba? It is about remembering what Yahweh did for our people, and it is about giving thanks," another of his sons added thoughtfully.

Elkanah's face softened and then glowed with pride. "Indeed, my wise son. It is a time to remember our covenant with Yahweh and to honor the traditions handed down from our forefathers."

The conversation continued with questions, answers, laughter, and memories. The younger boys listened intently to their older siblings. The older boys, in turn, shared moments they remembered best.

Then Eitan, the oldest son, cleared his throat. His voice held mischief. "Speaking of traditions, do you remember when Uncle Ephraim brought his new father-in-law's goats to the feast at Shiloh? He insisted they were sacred animals and tried to include them in the procession! What a fun prank!"

Laughter erupted around the table. With a chuckle, Eitan continued, "The goats had other ideas. They ran in all directions, scattering food baskets and knocking over tents. Uncle Ephraim was left chasing them, his robes flying, shouting blessings and apologies!"

Elkanah chuckled, shaking his head. "Yes, that was a feast to remember. But it reminds us that even in our most sacred moments, there is room for laughter and the unexpected ways Yahweh can touch our lives."

After the meal, Elkanah stood and gestured for the family to gather around. They always observed a unique tradition, a few simple songs passed down through the generations that they sang together to thank Yahweh for His blessings.

Elkanah began. His voice was solid and melodic. As the family joined him, their voices rose and fell in unison.

Yahweh, our Yahweh, the Keeper of our days,
Guide us, protect us, and show us Your ways.
With grateful hearts we sing Your praise
For love and mercy that never decays.
From Egypt's land You led us free
With a mighty hand and a guiding decree.
In Canaan's soil we plant and reap;
Your promises, O Lord, we joyfully keep.
Together we stand, as family, as friends;
Your covenant, O Yahweh, never breaks, never bends.
We raise our voices, a harmonious blend,
To You, our Maker, our Savior, our End.

The simple melody lingered, and Hannah closed her eyes. Elkanah began a second song, echoing the words of Miriam, a prophetess who sang of praise and triumph and whose words resonated through generations.

"Sing to Yahweh, for He has triumphed gloriously. He has thrown the horse and its rider into the sea! Yahweh is my strength and song. He has become my salvation. This is my Yahweh, and I will praise Him."

The lyrics filled the courtyard. And as Hannah's thoughts drifted to their upcoming journey to Shiloh, a spark lit within her as she pictured herself among the other choir members, voices lifted in unison, praising Yahweh. The sensation was like an old familiar friend as it bubbled up from her core, tingling through her limbs and causing her heart to beat faster in anticipation.

A smile tugged at the corners of her mouth, unbidden and genuine. She pictured the tabernacle, and a sense of awe washed over her. Even during her darkest days, going there always provided a unique peace, as if Yahweh's presence filled the air.

The wind picked up, stirring the olive leaves, and the song shifted to a higher key. As they sang of Yahweh's mighty deeds, something stirred within Hannah. It was the same feeling she had experienced previously at the tabernacle, a sensation of being touched by something divine, something beyond comprehension. She gasped, the suddenness of the feeling taking her breath away.

The song faltered, and everyone stared at her. The older boys looked at her with concern. Elkanah's gaze met hers, and in it she clearly saw a question she couldn't quite answer. The wind died down, but the sensation lingered, a whisper of something profound that promised change.

Hannah's heart pounded, and she reached for Elkanah's hand, seeking comfort. The feeling stirring within was elusive, but it left its mark. Something had changed, and she knew the journey to Shiloh would hold a significance she did not yet understand.

A knowing filled Elkanah's expression. Was this what her husband had been trying to tell her? Yes, they were journeying to Shiloh, but perhaps even now, Yahweh's hand was moving in ways they could not see.

CHAPTER FIVE

Hannah's feet carried her along the worn path to town, the earth firm beneath her sandals. The sun was warm on her shoulders, and the scent of blooming flowers mingled with the faint aroma of freshly baked bread coming from the closest homes. Spring had kissed the land with life.

In a different way than usual, the warmth seeped inside Hannah too this morning. It pushed out the winter's chill that had clung to her heart since those first years of marriage when, month after month, it became clear she would not be bearing a son to carry on her husband's legacy.

As she walked, she looked around at the lush landscapes and rolling hills of Ramah, where Elkanah's clan had settled. Her mind wandered to the first time she realized the honor afforded the wife of a prominent Levite. Elkanah's family's legacy had once filled her with pride—their wisdom, music, and spiritual guidance to the community. The watchers were the keepers of the faith, and she was part of it.

But as the years passed and her womb remained barren, the honor turned to disgrace. She could see it in the sidelong glances of the village women, hear it in the whispered prayers at the sanctuary, and feel it in the hollow emptiness that settled within her each night.

Her husband's melodies, once a source of joy, transformed into a melancholy tune to her ears. The same hands that played the lyre with such grace were the hands in which she wished to place a son.

The taste of the Passover meal, the texture of the unleavened bread, the aroma of the sacrificed lamb—all became bitter reminders of what she could not provide. Each ritual, song, and prayer was a thorn in her heart, pricking her with the painful reality that she was failing her husband, his legacy, and Yahweh.

As Hannah neared the town, she could hear children's laughter. She longed to see Elkanah's face glow with fatherly pride as he looked upon *their* child. More than anything, she wanted to know the warmth of a tiny hand clutching hers, a child that was born of her body.

Yet today, the laughter didn't pierce her as it once had. Through a restless night, she had even considered praying again. She was the wife of a Levite, yes, but she was also a woman who found it easier not to pray than to believe Yahweh heard her pleas and still withheld what she desired most.

The town's sights and sounds closed around her, but she felt adrift, lost in a sea of what could have been and was not to be. And as she continued walking, the weight of that legacy bore down on her, becoming a burden she carried with every step. A longing that echoed with every beat of her aching heart. And yet, somehow, she felt an almost imperceptible shift somewhere deep within her.

Hannah's feet kicked up dust as she approached Ayala's new home. The house was nestled among olive groves on a modest plot of land, constructed of sun-dried mud bricks and covered with a thatched roof.

Hannah knocked, and the heavy wooden door creaked open. The dear face of Ayala greeted her with a warm smile. "Hannah! Welcome, welcome! Come in."

Ayala's home was humble yet lively. The main room was adorned with simple woven rugs. Clay pots no doubt full of herbs and olives lined the shelves. A small fire crackled in the hearth, and a pot of stew bubbled gently. The sweet aroma of freshly baked bread filled the air, and a pang of nostalgia for her early days of marriage struck Hannah.

"It is lovely, Ayala," Hannah praised. "You have made it a true home."

Ayala's face, more akin to her father's thoughtful gaze than her mother's striking beauty, lit up with a shy blush. Her petite frame radiated a newfound grace, a silent testament to the contentment she found in marriage.

Ayala guided Hannah to a low wooden stool. "Here, try this bread. I baked it myself this morning."

The bread was warm in Hannah's hands, and as she bit into it, the taste and texture tugged at her heart, weaving a tapestry of nostalgia and pride for the young woman before her. The room resonated with the simple, caring details that spoke of Ayala's heart and character. Hannah knew that Ayala would thrive. She already appeared to be doing just that.

"You did well," Hannah whispered, her throat thick with emotion. If she had a daughter, this was what it would feel like.

Ayala's smile blossomed. "We are still settling in, but it feels right."

"Yes," Hannah said with understanding and affection. "It feels right."

As Hannah broke off a second piece of bread, her thoughts drifted back to Ayala's wedding three months prior. The ceremony had been a beautiful blend of tradition and young love. Elkanah had led Ayala to her waiting groom with his jaw set firm and eyes glistening with unshed tears as he placed Ayala's hand into Simeon's—a symbol of transferring his authority and protection to her new husband.

Peninnah had adorned her daughter with jewelry and fine linens, a testament to Ayala's purity and virtue. There was feasting and dancing with the entire community who came together to celebrate the sacred union.

Hannah watched from the sidelines with both joy and sorrow flowing through her. Though she cared for Ayala within her home and loved her as her own, she was not her mother. Hannah had sat apart, a silent observer of a moment that stirred memories of her own wedding day.

The ceremony ended with the groom carrying Ayala to their new home to start their new life together. It was then that Elkanah and Peninnah returned to their own house, and their roles toward Ayala shifted from daily caregivers to wise counselors, always available but no longer central.

Ayala's voice brought Hannah back to the present, and they continued to chat, sharing stories and laughter.

When Ayala mentioned the upcoming journey, Hannah said, "All my things are ready to go. Would you like me to help you pack?"

Ayala's face broke into a smile, and she nodded eagerly. "Yes, please. Your help would be most welcome."

They spent the next hour preparing for the journey, with their hands busy and their conversation flowing. They talked of family, the joys and struggles of daily life, and the latest news from their tribe. Laughter rang through the house as Ayala recounted the mishaps of learning to run her household, while Hannah shared her wisdom, guidance, and gentle teasing.

With practiced efficiency, Hannah helped Ayala pack the necessary items. They gathered the traditional unleavened bread and bitter herbs for the Passover Seder. The wine, an essential part of the celebration, was stored in a sealed leather flask.

Ayala carefully refolded her special shawl, woven with intricate patterns and vibrant colors, which she would wear during the festival. They also packed oil lamps, cooking utensils, and bedding, ensuring she had everything she and Simeon would need in Shiloh.

As they tucked more items into baskets and bags, Ayala looked up at Hannah, her eyes glistening with gratitude.

"Thank you, Hannah," she said softly, her voice full of emotion. "I do not know what I would do without you."

"We are family, dear girl." Hannah reached out and took Ayala's hands in her own. "We always support each other."

As she rose from her stool, Hannah's eyes were drawn to a delicately carved piece of wood that adorned the mantel. The carving depicted two hands entwined, a symbol of unity and love. "That is beautiful. Did your Simeon make it?"

Ayala nodded. "Yes, he is quite the craftsman. It is a symbol of our new beginning."

Hannah's gaze then settled on another carving, this one more intricate, displaying a bird in flight, its wings spread wide, every feather etched with meticulous detail. The bird seemed almost ready to take off from its wooden perch, full of life and grace.

"And this one?" Hannah asked, pointing to the carving. "Did Simeon make this too?"

Ayala's face softened, and she looked at the carving with affection and sadness. "Yes, he made it for my imma. He wanted to give her something beautiful."

Hannah didn't ask why the carving still sat on Ayala's shelf, but worry lines creased the young woman's face. "I hope she likes it," Ayala said, her voice tinged with apprehension.

Following Ayala's gaze, Hannah looked up and scoffed playfully, "How could she not like it?" She attempted to keep her tone light even as yesterday's events and Peninnah's mocking filled her mind.

Ayala shrugged. "You know my imma."

Hannah's smile faltered as she met Ayala's eyes. Yes, she knew Peninnah. She also understood the complexity of her relationship with her daughter. The unspoken tensions, the expectations, the misunderstandings played out in the silences, the glances, and the careful choosing of words.

Hannah reached out and placed a comforting hand on Ayala's shoulder. "Your imma loves you, Ayala. She may not always show it the way you want, but she loves you. And she will love whatever Simeon made for her."

Hannah took the carving from the shelf, wrapped it, and handed it to Ayala. Then she nodded toward one of the baskets Ayala packed. Peninnah would be celebrating a birthday in Shiloh. Hannah guessed Simeon had carved it to present to his new mother-in-law there.

Ayala's eyes welled with unshed tears as she set the wrapped carving to the side. Hannah's heart ached for the young woman.

"She is proud of you," Hannah whispered, her voice full of conviction. "And so am I."

Ayala wiped a tear that managed to break free. Then she nodded and offered a soft smile, accepting Hannah's words.

The two women resumed their work, the unspoken knowing between them deepening. They understood each other in ways others could not, their shared experiences binding them together.

As they packed the last basket, Ayala's hand lingered on the wrapped package. Hannah watched her, sensing the turmoil within.

Finally, Ayala looked up, her eyes meeting Hannah's, a silent plea in her gaze. Hannah nodded, understanding the unspoken request, and Ayala placed the package in the basket. She would be there for Ayala, guiding, supporting, and loving her as she could.

Hannah's mind returned to a conversation with Peninnah, who had mentioned that Ayala was unwell. "Your imma said you were under the weather yesterday?"

Ayala immediately waved off the concern. "Oh, it was nothing. Just a minor ailment. I am so glad you came." She paused, a shadow crossing her face. "I was worried about my imma's visit. I remember how she used to get before our trips to Shiloh, frustrated about so many things."

She looked down. "I used to pretend that you were my imma, Hannah. I do not understand my own. We are so different." Her eyes welled with unspoken emotion. "She does not always say kind things about Simeon. 'He is just a carpenter,' she says. 'You deserve more.' But I have never wanted anything more than a simple home. I think my imma wanted me to have what she never got."

Hannah didn't understand. "What do you mean?"

"I suppose you would not know unless my abba or imma told you," Ayala said, her voice softening. "Imma told me she thought she would be the bride of a wealthy merchant's son from a neighboring town. Yet in the end, he chose another. It was not long after that that her father met my father. It was not what my imma wanted, but by this time, she had been waiting for years to get married. And in the end, she chose not to be alone."

The words crashed against Hannah, leaving her stunned and silent. She had never seen great love between Elkanah and Peninnah, and though she tried not to speculate, Ayala's revelation was unsettling. Peninnah had thought Elkanah better than being alone. What type of relationship was that? Hannah's heart ached. Elkanah was an honest, kind, and fair man, and any women should feel blessed to be by his side. *And yet*, she reminded herself, *marriages are usually based on practical concerns.* This new knowledge shouldn't surprise her.

She sat quietly, not knowing what to say, the room heavy with the weight of unspoken emotions and truths. Finally, she found her voice, choosing to speak from her heart.

"I am thankful your imma joined our family." Hannah looked into Ayala's eyes, hoping the young woman saw her love and sincerity. "You, Ayala, are one of the greatest joys of my life—"

Before the words were completely out of Hannah's mouth, Ayala leaned in for an embrace and tucked her head under Hannah's chin just as she had done when she was a child. Hannah hugged Ayala tighter, the emptiness of her arms easing slightly.

After a few minutes, Ayala pulled back, her lips pressed into a thin line. "Thank you for always being there."

"You are family," Hannah replied, her voice filled with affection. "I will always be here for you, no matter what."

Ayala's eyes flashed with something unreadable, and her smile seemed forced. "I know, and I am so grateful for that. You have been the mother I needed. And still do."

Hannah sensed that Ayala wanted to say something more. But she didn't want to push. Whatever it was, Ayala would share it when she was ready. "You are a strong and loving woman," Hannah reassured her, placing a gentle hand on Ayala's shoulder. "I am proud to know you."

Ayala smiled and nodded. "Thank you, Hannah."

As the sun began to dip, casting a golden glow through the narrow windows, Hannah glanced outside and realized the time. "I must be going, dear one. Tomorrow will be a long day on the road."

Ayala's expression flickered with hesitation as though she were again on the verge of saying something. But then she embraced Hannah warmly, thanking her again for the visit and the help. "See you tomorrow, and may Yahweh bless you."

"You as well. Take care," Hannah said as she returned the embrace.

With a final smile and wave, Hannah stepped out into the cooling afternoon. Her mind was overflowing with thoughts of the upcoming journey and the sense that something was weighing on Ayala—something other than her relationship with Peninnah. Hannah wished she could help, but she knew some things had to be worked out in their own time.

As Hannah made her way home, with her heart full of anticipation and concern, she whispered a prayer for Ayala and Simeon, asking that whatever was troubling Ayala would be resolved soon. She longed to ease the young woman's burdens.

CHAPTER SIX

The warm scent of the soil filled Hannah's nostrils as she walked along the road toward home. A few dozen families of men, women, and servants worked diligently, piling their supplies outside their doorways. Children scurried about, their laughter ringing.

Yet the laughter couldn't mask the underlying tension. In years past, the road to Shiloh would have been busy with far more pilgrims—faithful families traveling to worship and make offerings. Once, faith in Yahweh had been strong and the village was united.

But times had changed. Far fewer people were making the trek now. Some openly refused to go to the place where Eli was allowing his wicked sons to do evil. These sons, Hophni and Phinehas, were men of greed and lust, using their authority as priests to extort from the people. They were known for taking the best of the sacrificed meat for themselves before giving the leftovers to Yahweh.

So many had abandoned the Lord's ways, turning to the Canaanite gods. The idols were a symptom of a loss of direction. Her people no longer were a united clan under Yahweh's guidance.

Hannah felt a pang of sadness as she thought about the spiritual decay. The village had lost its way. The innocence and purity of her childhood faith seemed distant and unattainable. Yet was she any better? No. Although she believed in Yahweh, she could not murmur one more prayer only to have it be unanswered.

Would her people ever find their way back to Yahweh? Would she? Or would they continue to drift, lost and searching, pulled further away from the path of righteousness by the allure of false gods, the disappointment of lost dreams, and the corruption of once-holy men?

But today those worries moved to the back of Hannah's mind. Even though nothing had changed in their community, something felt a little bit different inside of her.

Usually, Hannah kept her head down, eyes trained on her feet and the hard-packed path, avoiding the other women. She would focus on the rhythm of her footsteps, the soft rustle of her garments, and the distant sounds of village life, all to escape their silent speculation.

Today she made eye contact with the women and smiled instead of looking away. The bright faces and innocent joy of the excitement over their yearly pilgrimage touched her. It wasn't that her longing disappeared or that her situation changed. Her arms were still empty, her home still void of the joyful sounds of her own children. But something deep within her had begun to shift.

As Hannah passed a home close to the roadway, she saw the family gathered in the courtyard, surrounded by bags, bundles of clothing, and clay pots carrying grain and oil. The sun cast a golden glow on the scene, highlighting the flushed cheeks of the children as they attempted to help their parents with the packing.

Yonah glanced up from securing a bag of what were probably lentils. Hannah and Yonah had become young brides around the same time, and for a while, they were close, sharing dreams, hopes, and the excitement of starting their new lives. They spent countless afternoons together, discussing everything from their favorite recipes to their husbands' quirks. They laughed and cried together, their hearts knit in the unique bond of being newly married.

But as the years went by, Yonah's family grew. Hannah's remained just her and Elkanah, and a distance crept between their friendship. The conversations became more infrequent, the visits shorter, and the once easy laughter was replaced with polite smiles. Hannah often wondered when exactly they began to drift apart. Was it after Yonah's first child? Or second?

Yonah's eyes widened as she spotted Hannah. Her face brightened in surprise at Hannah's wave.

"Hannah! Blessed be your day!" Yonah called. "Is it just me, or does the packing multiply overnight?"

"It must be a blessing from above, testing our readiness for the journey. But you know us, always up to the challenge!"

Yonah nodded and sighed. "We have been preparing for weeks, but it always feels like a rush at the end."

"It is the same for us. But the journey and the celebration make it all worth it."

Yonah's eyes twinkled. "Yes, we would not have it any other way, would we?"

"No, we would not." Hannah lingered for a moment, feeling the warmth of the sun on her face and the reconnection with Yonah.

"Mama, is Leeba's Hannah coming to Shiloh with us?" asked Yonah's young daughter. Her face was smeared with dirt, and her eyes shone with innocence.

Leeba's Hannah. Hannah's heart pattered. She wasn't Leeba's mother, but the term acknowledged they were family. *Almost like an imma,* Hannah thought to herself.

"Yes, dear one, we all journey together as Yahweh's chosen people." Yonah's voice was gentle.

The little girl, Tamar, was a delightful and curious child. Her chestnut hair was tied into playful braids, and her cheeks were flushed with excitement. She wore a simple linen dress that swayed as she moved. Her tiny feet danced impatiently, and the air around her brimmed with energy.

A lump in Hannah's throat grew, seeing in Tamar the hope and promise for the future of their people. "Indeed, little one." Hannah paused and bent down to meet the girl's gaze. "We will sing songs and tell stories along the way. It will be a time of joy and celebration."

Tamar clapped her hands in delight, and Yonah's eyes met Hannah's. A shared understanding passed between them. In Tamar's joy, they were reminded that all the work was worth it so that the next generation could learn Yahweh's ways.

"May Yahweh bless your journey," Yonah said sincerely, her hand resting on her daughter's head. "May He fill your heart with peace and joy."

Hannah's eyes welled with tears at the kindness in Yonah's words. "Thank you. May He bless you and your family as well." She couldn't help but feel a pang of longing for the closeness she and Yonah once shared. But she also felt grateful that friendships could still be rekindled, no matter how long it had been.

Hannah continued with a final wave. And as she strode away, a new thought filled her mind. What if the women in the town hadn't been looking upon her with shame? What if they simply didn't know what to say to her as their families grew?

The thought was like a balm to Hannah's wounded spirit. And as she continued her walk home, a weight lifted from her shoulders. The world seemed brighter, more vibrant, and filled with possibilities she hadn't allowed herself to see.

At this moment, she no longer felt like just a woman longing for a child, which had been her reality for so many years. Today, she was a daughter of Israel, about to embark on a sacred quest.

Hannah arrived home to find Peninnah and the servants in a whirlwind of activity, organizing and packing. As she approached, the sounds of laughter, chatter, and clinking pottery filled her ears. The servants moved to and fro, each one assigned a specific task. Some packed clay pots that contained olive oil, wine, or grain, while others secured bundles of clothing, utensils, and necessary tools into the wagon.

Wooden wheels creaked under the weight of the provisions being loaded. Hannah paused to watch. Despite their differences, she couldn't deny Peninnah's ability to manage the household and these preparations. The scents of leather, spices, and freshly baked bread mingled in the air.

Peninnah worked with one hand while the baby slept in a sling against her chest, and her instructions to the servants were clear and precise. There was a rhythm to her actions, born of years of experience.

A servant girl rushed past Hannah, carrying a bundle of unleavened baked barley bread. Its warm, yeasty aroma wafted through the air.

"Mind the bread, Adi!" Peninnah called after the girl. Her voice carried a note of amusement. "We do not want it trampled before we leave!"

Adi giggled, looking over her shoulder. "No, Mistress Peninnah! It will be safe, I promise!"

Hannah's eyes landed on the packed items—the familiar household necessities and the ceremonial objects required for Passover rituals. Her heart swelled with pride and nostalgia as she observed the care and reverence with which these items were handled. The memories of past pilgrimages, the songs, the prayers, and the shared experiences continued to flood back.

Finally, Peninnah's sharp eyes caught Hannah's, and her voice cut through the noise, dripping with condescension. "Have you a problem, Hannah? Do you find our preparations lacking?"

Instead of cowering or walking away, Hannah met Peninnah's gaze steadily. "Not at all," she replied. "I was just admiring your organizational skills. Everything seems to be in perfect order."

Peninnah's eyes widened and then narrowed, assessing Hannah's sincerity. After a moment, she said grudgingly, "Well, someone has to keep this chaos at bay."

Her words struck Hannah with a realization. Giving birth to one baby after another must have been hard on Peninnah. The complicated pregnancies, the many children to care for. Hannah had never stopped to consider these things before, since she'd been so enmeshed in her own cares.

She bent down to help Peninnah with a bundle of linens, her hands brushing against the soft, well-worn fabric. As she worked beside the younger woman, she couldn't help but see her in a new light.

Peninnah looked weary, her face marked by lines that spoke of stress and fatigue. Her body carried extra weight from birthing babies, and gray had begun to streak her temples. Dark circles shadowed her eyes. Hannah wondered if the baby still woke to be fed at night. With a pang of guilt, she realized she didn't know the answer because she never asked.

"I never thanked you properly," Hannah said, her voice tinged with regret, "for all you do for this family, for the children. It has...it has not gone unnoticed."

Peninnah's eyes darted toward Hannah and then looked away. "I do what I must, Hannah. Just as you do."

A silence fell between them. Hannah's mind wandered to Ayala, and a fresh wave of guilt washed over her. Ayala had sent a servant asking her mother not to come, yet the young woman welcomed Hannah with open arms this morning. How would Peninnah feel if she knew?

Hannah had always had a special bond with Ayala, mostly because she'd had more time to pay attention to the girl, to sit and listen, and to teach her about caring for a home. It wasn't Peninnah's fault that she couldn't do those things with all the other children to care for.

"Peninnah," Hannah began, hesitating, "I have been blind to many things. Your sacrifices, your strength. I have been wrapped up in my pain, but now I see I have missed so much."

Peninnah's face softened further, and the weariness lifted from her eyes. "We all have our burdens, Hannah. We all have our blind spots."

They worked silently for a moment, the shared task bridging the gap between them. Finally, the women's preparations were nearly complete. There would be last-minute details to attend to after dinner. Elkanah and the older boys would yoke the oxen in the morning and load the Passover lamb.

Hannah felt an unexpected blanket of peace settle over her. Their family was on the path that Yahweh laid before them. Perhaps the trip to Shiloh was just what they needed to unite their family—Hannah and Peninnah in particular—and grow in Yahweh's love.

CHAPTER SEVEN

The dusky light of the sinking sun bathed their home in a honeyed glow. Hannah set the last dish on the table. From the back courtyard, the older boys played and called to each other with youthful exuberance—their laughter echoed like sweet melodies just beyond the clay-brick home.

Hannah should have called them in to dinner. Instead, she paused and watched Elkanah play with his sons. The sound of children at play had often been a source of pain for her. Tonight, it was different. Tonight, she allowed herself to enjoy their fun without letting it pull her into despair.

Peninnah was seated across the room after putting the baby to bed. The younger woman's face was drawn, and her lips were pressed tightly together. Peninnah's eyes were distant, lost in thoughts that Hannah could only guess. But something in her expression made Hannah's heart catch. Could it be that Peninnah had noticed the renewed tenderness between Elkanah and Hannah as of late? The thought sent a thrill of both guilt and satisfaction through her, but she pushed it aside. Whether the fragile truce they forged an hour ago would survive, Hannah didn't know. But she was seeing Peninnah in a new light.

Hannah's gaze returned to her husband, and she marveled at how he interacted with his children. They were not her flesh and blood, but Hannah cared for them too. Did they feel her love? She had been going through the motions for so long.

As she pondered this, her gaze was drawn to three women beyond where Elkanah and the children played. They were headed toward the fields, baskets in hand. Surely they were out to pick bitter herbs. Something stirred within her—a tentative connection to her neighbors and their shared faith despite the village's struggles.

Without a second thought, she hurried outside and guided the women to the best spot on Elkanah's property where the herbs grew in abundance. They exchanged grateful glances and soft words of thanks, and Hannah felt a warmth in her heart.

With a final wave, she returned home, cheeks flushed with exertion and embarrassment at her impulsiveness.

Hannah hurried into the dining area where the family had taken seats around the table for the evening meal, a time-honored tradition before the journey to Shiloh. Her step quickened at the thought of the rituals that lay ahead.

Peninnah was already serving the simple but hearty feast of lentil stew, fresh bread, and a few olives. Elkanah looked up as she entered, clearly concerned. "Wherever did you go just now?"

"I am sorry," she replied, catching her breath. "Some of our neighbors were walking by. They carried baskets, searching for the bitter herbs. I showed them where ours grew and offered them."

Elkanah's eyes widened with surprise and approval. "It is good you did so. We must encourage the faithful ones among us."

Hannah nodded and approached the table next to where Peninnah stood with the dish of lentils in hand.

Clearing his throat, Elkanah motioned Peninnah to sit while Hannah served the meal.

Hannah shook her head. "That is not necessary." Her voice was gentle but firm. "Peninnah can do it."

Surprise flashed on Elkanah's face, quickly replaced by understanding. He nodded.

As Peninnah began to serve, Hannah took her usual place at the table, her heart feeling strangely light. The familiar ache of longing was still there, but a newfound clarity and empathy now accompanied it. She looked around at this family, appreciating the simple joy of being together. Even amid uncertainty and sorrow, they were connected by their history, faith, and Yahweh's mighty hand.

The boys had taken their places. Their cheeks were still flushed with the excitement of their earlier game. Leeba, just three years old, sat on a bench, short legs dangling above the ground. She watched her brothers' every move. Curls framed her round face, bouncing slightly as she turned her head, following the activity in the room.

Hannah remembered little Tamar's words, *Leeba's Hannah.* A soft smile lifted her lips at the memory. Hannah enjoyed her time with Leeba, cherishing their shared moments of laughter and discovery. But their relationship was different from the deep bond she had with Ayala. Perhaps both she and Peninnah had made sure of that, consciously or unconsciously.

There was a bittersweet tinge to Hannah's feelings as she looked at Leeba, a combination of love, longing, and a subtle acknowledgment of the existing boundaries. But these thoughts were soon swept away as the family joined hands.

Taking the hand of Elkanah on one side and Leeba on the other, Hannah joined the family's voices as they were raised in a song of gratitude and hope, echoing the timeless traditions of their ancestors. A reverent calm replaced the boys' playful laughter. Elkanah led the singing, his strong voice guiding the melody, while the rest of the family chimed in, filling the room with sweet harmony.

Oh, Yahweh, guide our way
As we journey to Your holy place.
With grateful hearts and trusting grace,
We seek Your face in Shiloh's embrace.
Through valleys deep and mountains high,
Your love sustains, Your hand is nigh.
In Passover's shadow, we shall find
Redemption's song and peace of mind.
For ancestors' faith and lessons learned,
Your mighty hand and the freedom earned,
We sing Your praise and humbly pray,
Oh, Yahweh, guide our way.

The words were handed down through generations, a prayer for guidance, protection, and blessing. The voices filled the room, uniting them all, young and old, in a moment of shared faith and love.

Peninnah's eyes were soft, her voice surprisingly gentle as she harmonized with the others. The children's faces, usually lit with the glint of mischief, were serene and focused, as if they understood the significance of the song and the journey ahead.

A lump filled Hannah's throat as they finished the song. The last note lingered, a hauntingly beautiful reminder of their purpose. Moments later, as they ate, she allowed her mind to drift to the coming journey to Shiloh, a place of worship and sacrifice, where the Ark of the Covenant resided. For those who still believed, the pilgrimage was a family event and a communal expression of faith, reaffirming their covenant with Yahweh.

The path ahead might have challenges, but Hannah also knew their faith would guide them just as it had guided their ancestors. With a contented sigh, she reached for a piece of bread and tasted the familiar flavor of home.

In the cooling night, under a sky dotted with countless stars, they were connected to a heritage that had endured for generations, grounded in a belief that was as unshakable as the rock fortresses hovering over their village.

Yet the peace of the evening meal was a fleeting moment, soon shattered by the need to make the final frantic preparations.

Peninnah's snapping dialogue overshadowed this profound connection, her temper flaring as she rushed through their home once the meal was finished.

"Move faster, boys! Your robes, where are your robes?" Peninnah's voice was sharp, echoing through the rooms. "Hannah, have you seen their sandals? How can you just stand there?"

Hannah looked up from where she was folding spare bedding. Her heart sank at Peninnah's anger. Their truce had come to an end, then. Hannah rose, trying to keep her voice calm. "I will help you look."

"You always say that, but what help are you, really?"

Knowing it would do no one any good to provoke Peninnah, Hannah simply said, "We will get this done together."

Peninnah paused. Her eyes narrowed as she regarded Hannah. Then, with a huff, she continued her frenzied packing, but her tone was slightly less sharp. "Fine, just make sure we have enough unleavened bread. I asked the servants to make more. You know how the boys eat."

Hannah moved to the shelf in the kitchen where loaves of bread cooled. The freshly baked unleavened bread, a reminder of the haste in which their ancestors fled Egypt, had just finished baking. She worked with the servants to carefully wrap the loaves and place them in woven baskets.

Never mind that the servants were familiar with the routine since they made the same journey for the holy celebrations three times a year.

But Hannah's thoughts returned to Peninnah's worn face and sharp words. The new light in which she was beginning to see Peninnah grew a bit brighter. Hannah's own role in this family grew clearer as well, as understanding unfolded. They were a family. All of them, including Hannah. And they were bound together by ritual and tradition, by real struggles and joys. And unlike other families who turned their attention to false gods, at least they strove to honor their faith. Honoring each other was sometimes more difficult. But Hannah found herself pledging herself to try.

Just as the last of their items were packed and covered with a heavy tarp, a soft spring rain fell outside. Inside, where it was dry, Elkanah sat on a rough-hewn wooden stool and lit an oil lamp. The dim glow cast a warm, flickering light across the room. Even though it was nearing bedtime, his children did not move toward their sleeping quarters. Instead, the boys and Leeba gathered around him, their faces rapt with curiosity.

Even as the children settled, Peninnah paced restlessly, her movements sharp and erratic, causing the younger children to glance up with apprehension. With barely a glance at her husband, Peninnah moved to the kitchen, where the servants had brought more items from the earthen cellar.

"Why did you just bring these now? I told you we needed extra olives! Now we must remember to pack them tomorrow," Peninnah snapped. Her words were like a whip, causing a palpable tension. "How many times must I repeat myself?"

The servants hurried to obey her commands in a flurry of activity. The men had already fenced in the unblemished lambs for sacrifice—one for their family and more for other families who had arrived today to purchase them from Elkanah.

A distant rumble of thunder accentuated the woman's mood, and the room seemed to tremble in response to Peninnah's increasing distress. The children shifted uncomfortably, glancing at their father and then to Hannah, seeking reassurance.

Without warning, Peninnah stopped and pressed a hand to her temple, her face contorted in pain.

"I need to lie down," she finally announced, her voice suddenly soft and weary. "I have a terrible headache."

Hannah stood and faced her husband, speaking gently, "I will be happy to help with the children tonight."

Elkanah looked up at her, gratitude in his eyes. "Thank you, Hannah."

A collective sigh seemed to escape the room as Peninnah left. Hannah couldn't help but notice the children exchange relieved glances.

Leeba tugged at Elkanah's robe. "Abba, tell us a story?"

Elkanah smiled, his eyes twinkling. "Of course, my little dove. Gather around, and I shall tell you a tale from our ancestors."

CHAPTER EIGHT

The flickering oil lamp caught in the depth of Elkanah's dark eyes. His hand, as firm as it was gentle, ruffled the hair of Leeba, who was sitting next to him. The cherubic girl had inherited her abba's expressive eyes. When Hannah heard the baby crying, she asked Shifrah to bring the baby to them. Elkanah placed the boy on his knee.

While Hannah maintained a close relationship with Ayala, she kept distant from Peninnah's other children. Yet this youngest one, Tobiah, who was nearly a year old, made resisting hard. He was plump and happy. Even now, as Peninnah rested and tended to the ache in her head, Tobiah reached for Hannah with a balled fist.

Hannah leaned closer and pretended to nibble on the baby's curled fingers. "As tasty as manna," she said. The boy's high and light laughter caused his body to bounce. Elkanah's deep laughter joined in.

There was no need for words. After two decades together, it seemed she and Elkanah had come to an unspoken new understanding over the last couple of days to accept what was. While there was still an ache of longing for a child, Hannah no longer had the same stabbing pain. She had prayed and cried enough for a lifetime.

"Am I still good if I do not bless you and Elkanah with a child?"
She could almost hear Yahweh's whisper as if He spoke aloud.
Yet it was not an audible voice but rather an echo of the wind.
She tilted her body toward the open doorway, hoping to hear
more. But the voice was gone.

"Is something wrong?" her husband asked.

"I think it is just the noise of the other families filling their
wagons," she said. It was the truth, but she didn't tell her husband there was something more too.

Elkanah nodded and reminded his sons of their roles once
they reached Shiloh—sharing a story of the first time he worked
alongside his abba and accidentally caught the hem of his robe
on fire.

The children laughed, and there was a pang in her heart, a
familiar twinge that reminded her of the absence she felt. The
longing to bear a son to work alongside Elkanah at the tabernacle was never far from her mind, a desire unfulfilled and yet
tempered by a deeper understanding and acceptance. Yahweh
had other plans for her, and though the path was painful, she
was coming to find peace in it.

The children's growing laughter pulled her from her rev-
erie, and she smiled. She had no child, but she had experienced
Yahweh's goodness in other ways, hadn't she? Her husband was
kind to her, and they had their health.

Then a sense of profound gratitude swelled within Hannah.
Her husband was a man of Yahweh and the man of her heart.
He was as a pillar of strength in their home just as he was in
the tabernacle. On the good days, like today, she remembered

this. And thankfully, on the bad days, when she found her emotions being pulled down into the darkness once more, Elkanah showed compassion and understanding.

Tomorrow, Elkanah would again don the priestly attire. His countenance would take on the solemnity befitting a man serving the Almighty. But tonight, he was theirs—a husband, a father, a man in love with his family and Yahweh.

Elkanah handed the sleepy baby back to the servant. The lamp flickered, its warm glow illuminating the lines etched deep into his weathered face. Beside him, Ya'akov, the second youngest boy, nearly ten, gazed up at his abba.

"Tell us another story, Abba," Ya'akov pleaded.

Elkanah smiled with affection. "Ah, young ones, gather close, and I shall take you back to the days of our ancestors, to the time of the Kohathites."

The boys leaned in. A servant made a fire in the hearth behind them.

"In the days of old," Elkanah began, "our forefather Kohath was the son of Levi, one of the twelve sons of Jacob. They were the chosen people of the Almighty, entrusted with the sacred duty of carrying the holy tent and all its furnishings through the wilderness." As the night deepened and the rain subsided, Elkanah began to weave the story. His voice was a calming melody.

The fire crackled and popped as the flames danced, creating an almost mystical ambiance around them.

"Kohath was a man of great wisdom and devotion," Elkanah continued. "He taught his sons the ways of the Lord and passed down the sacred responsibilities from generation to generation. The Kohathites were honored to transport the most sacred objects from the tent—the Ark of the Covenant, the Table of Showbread, the Menorah, and the Altar of Incense."

The young boy nodded. Even at this young age, Ya'akov knew the significance of those holy items.

"These sacred vessels were no ordinary objects, my children," Elkanah said solemnly. "They represent the very presence of the Almighty among His chosen people. The Ark, in particular, holds the stone tablets inscribed with the Ten Commandments— a testament to the covenant between Yahweh and our people, the Israelites."

"Why were the Kohathites chosen, Abba?" Oren, the second oldest boy, asked. He knew the answer, but asking the questions was part of the storytelling.

Elkanah leaned forward, clearly pleased at his son's perception. "Because, my dear ones, the Kohathites were known for their reverence and purity of heart. They were set apart to handle the holiest objects with utmost care and respect. As they traveled through the wilderness, they sang psalms and offered prayers, creating a spiritual shield around the tabernacle."

The fire's warmth intensified, mirroring the children's growing fascination.

"Your ancestors took pride in their sacred duty, knowing they were not merely carrying physical items but a symbol of Yahweh's guidance and protection," Elkanah said. "They were entrusted with a divine mission, and their unwavering faith strengthened the entire community of Israel."

Oren nodded. He clearly understood the significance of his father's words.

"Remember," Elkanah concluded, his voice gentle but firm, "the legacy of the Kohathites lives within us. Let their devotion and reverence inspire your faith journey as you grow."

The boys nodded. Eitan took Leeba in his arms, and she curled up and fell asleep. As the evening wore on, Elkanah shared more stories of the Kohathites and their unwavering commitment to Yahweh's call.

The servants had gone to bed. The flames of the fire started to die down, but Hannah stirred them, bringing them to life once more.

"Abba, tell us again about the Philistines," the third eldest son, Abiram, asked, his voice tinged with fear and fascination.

"Ah, the Philistines, the Sea Peoples, invaders from the islands in the north." Elkanah's voice had dropped to a conspiratorial whisper. "Even our great ancestor Abraham had dealings with them."

Elkanah began to spin the tale, his words painting a vivid picture of a fearsome and fascinating people.

"They settled in the region long ago, these Philistines, and they were a people like no other. They wore feathered headdresses, bright and colorful, a symbol of their strength and prowess. And around their necks, they wore guards to protect the backs of their heads, held by chin straps, a mark of their battle readiness."

Hannah could see from their faces that the boys' imaginations took flight, their minds filled with images of warriors, resplendent in their unique armor, fierce and determined.

"But why did they come here, Abba?" Zemir asked.

Elkanah's face grew grave, and he looked into the distance as if seeing the past unfold before his eyes. "They were a restless people, driven by a desire for new lands, new opportunities. They sailed across the sea, their ships carrying warriors and families, their eyes fixed on the horizon and their hearts set on conquest."

He paused, no doubt remembering those times.

"They were not all bad, these Philistines," Elkanah continued, his voice now soft and thoughtful. "They brought with them knowledge and skills, art, and culture. They built cities, they traded with our people, and they became a part of the fabric of this land."

"But they were also fierce in battle," Abiram, the third eldest son, said excitedly. "They fought with swords and spears, and they were feared by all who faced them."

Elkanah nodded, his face grave. "Yes, they were warriors, skilled and fearless. But they were also human, with hopes, dreams, families, and homes. They were not so different from us."

He looked at his children, his eyes showing the wisdom born of experience and understanding. "We must learn from the past, from the stories of those who came before us. Like the great Samson, there are times we must defeat our enemy lest they invade and attempt to make our people worship their gods—this, my sons, we must not allow this to happen."

Hannah stood at a distance. Elkanah's words resonated deeply within her, echoing the lessons she had learned at her abba's knee. She remembered when she was a child, full of innocence and dreams, listening to tales of faith, courage, and the constant battle to preserve their way of life.

As she looked at Elkanah's children, her heart ached with the knowledge that they too would face trials and tribulations. The Philistine threat was never far away, a shadow lurking at the edges of their peaceful existence. Would the fears and worries of attacks mar their childhood? Would they grow up with a sense of impending danger?

But she also knew that they were not alone. Their community was strong. There were still those among them bound by faith and a shared commitment to Yahweh's way. They were surrounded by people who understood the importance of unity, of standing firm against those who would try to lead them astray.

She thought of her neighbors, friends, and those within their community who lived with a quiet but unshakable faith. They were not warriors like Samson, but they fought their daily battles in how they lived their lives, and they endeavored to instill their faith in their children.

Hannah felt a surge of pride and love. Elkanah was one of those warriors of faith, a leader within their family and community. He understood the delicate balance of strength and compassion, of standing firm without losing sight of love and humanity.

With the children gathered around, she felt her sense of hope grow. Yes, there were challenges ahead, enemies to face, both physical and spiritual. But they were strong, they were united, and Yahweh guided them.

She was not their imma, but she could help Elkanah plant seeds of faith—seeds that could grow and flourish. And someday, this faith would be their shield and strength.

As Elkanah's story climaxed, Hannah felt a surge of gratitude. Their eyes met, and a world of understanding passed between them. A smile played on Elkanah's lips, reaching his eyes and touching Hannah's soul. She returned the smile, her heart swelling with love.

Another story ended. The children clapped, and Elkanah rose to his feet, moving toward Hannah. She welcomed him with open arms, feeling his strength, his love. She had given Elkanah no son, yet she was whole, and he thought her so. Their embrace was quick, but it was enough.

With their story time over, the children hurried to bed, the elder ones helping the younger ones. Elkanah returned to his stool and sat in quiet reflection. For a moment, Hannah remembered what it had been like when it was just the two of them, young and full of dreams for their future. Elkanah must have been thinking of it too.

"No matter what darkness we face in the days to come, we lift our voices." Elkanah's voice smoothed, and Hannah knew he was about to sing. "Like Miriam and Deborah, we rejoice. For Yahweh is with us, our strength and guide. In Him, we find refuge. In Him, we confide."

Hannah closed her eyes and allowed her husband's words to flow over her. The song was one he had written in their first few years of marriage. Then she joined in.

Sing a song of victory, oh, let it ring;
Our Yahweh is faithful, His praises we sing.
In His mighty hands we find our peace;
He brings deliverance and release.

Through parted waters, He made a way;
Miriam danced, her tambourine did sway.
In our struggles, we will trust and obey,
For in His presence we will find our way.

Sing a song of victory, oh, let it ring;
Our Yahweh is faithful, His praises we sing.
In His mighty hands we find our peace;
He brings deliverance and release.

Though the battle rages, we will not fear,
For our Yahweh is near, His voice we hear.
With hearts united we will stand as one;
In His strength we will overcome, we will overcome.

Deborah's courage, her wisdom renowned,
With faith and boldness she wore a crown.
In our weakness His power is displayed.
Through every trial His grace won't fade.

Sing a song of victory, oh, let it ring;
Our Yahweh is faithful, His praises we sing.

In His mighty hands we find our peace;
He brings deliverance and release.

So let us sing like Miriam and Deborah,
With hearts ablaze let us praise forever.
For our Yahweh is faithful, His love profound,
Through Him true victory is found.

As the song ended, Elkanah rose. He took her shawl from the hook and led them down the moonlit path toward the rock tower. Did the watchman look down on them and wonder what they were doing on a stroll at such an hour? Hannah guessed that he did, but she didn't worry about it. She felt a closer bond with her husband than she had in many years.

When they reached the top of a rise, they stood together in the waning twilight. The world was bathed in a palette of purples and blues, the end of one day heralding the uncertain promise of the next. The olive trees swayed gently in the distance.

"I will pray with you," Elkanah said softly, his voice a comforting balm to her weary soul. "We will ask the Lord together, Hannah. He will hear us."

His words were a pledge, a covenant, a reassurance that they were not alone in their suffering. Hannah's heart trembled, the aching void momentarily filled with Elkanah's steadfast faith.

Her throat tightened with emotion, so much that she could not speak. Ever since their early days of marriage, the watchtower, constructed of uncut stones, had stood as a monument.

It was a reminder that Yahweh was a strong fortress. That the Yahweh of their abbas was there for them too.

Elkanah led Hannah to sit on a log beneath one of the trees in the ancient olive grove. She traced the grooves of its bark with her fingers.

The gnarled branches above her whispered as they swayed in the night breeze. Each leaf cast intricate shadows in the soft moonlight. Elkanah breathed out a contented sigh as he sat beside her.

"Do you remember, Hannah?" His voice rose with the rich fragrance of freshly pressed olives. "Do you remember the first time I came to meet your abba right here in this olive grove?"

Her soul stirred to life with memories, shadows of the past that played in her mind. The young woman she had been. The young man Elkanah had been. Both were full of love, hopes, and dreams for a future overflowing with joy and children's laughter.

Elkanah pointed down the hill to the olive press. "Your abba spoke of marriage as a time of pressing. 'The strongest faith does not come from easy times but from pressing times. The same is true for love.' Those words have stayed with me."

Hannah's eyes were drawn to the olive press. She could make out its form under the moonlight. It was a solid structure with heavy wooden beams and a large stone wheel. Harvesters placed olives in a shallow basin, and the wheel would turn, crushing them under its weight. The pressure extracted the precious oil. The process was both violent and beautiful.

Emotions welled up within her. She could almost taste the fresh olives and feel the oily texture. Longing for her abba's gentleness and her imma's care filled her too. Both had left this earth within years of her marriage. A tear escaped, trailing down Hannah's cheek, mingling with the sweet taste of nostalgia.

"For the last decade, my love, it feels as if we have been walking two different paths," Elkanah said. "But I see it as a pressing time. We still have faith, and we still have love. It is time for us to come together in prayer again."

Hannah's heart trembled, caught between hope and despair. The thought of praying for a child filled her with longing and dread.

"Hannah," Elkanah urged, reaching out to take her hand, his touch familiar and electrifying, "I have received word that you have been invited to be part of the choir in Shiloh. Think of it, my love, singing praises to the Lord during the Passover." The news resonated within her, a spark of hope igniting.

How could she worship Yahweh without trusting Him? The scent of olives lingered in the air, a reminder of the past and a promise for the future.

"This is good news," she whispered. Was she speaking of the choir, or praying together? By Elkanah's firm grip on her hands, he took it as both.

"Let us pray together," he said, his face illuminated by the gentle moonlight. "Let us trust in His plan, in His time, and in His way."

Overhead, the stars pricked the darkening sky. The air still smelled of rain, and the ground was damp as they knelt together. Elkanah's hands wrapped around Hannah's again. Hannah whispered in agreement as her husband pleaded for understanding of Yahweh's ways, for strength, and for the blessing of a child.

As they cried out to the heavens, their prayers became like the river Jordan after a heavy rain. Hannah's tears mingled with her petitions. When her husband wiped his face and sniffled, she knew he'd cried too—the salt of human suffering seeking divine compassion.

Hannah wasn't sure how much time passed, but as they lifted their bent heads, their faces were wet but their hearts were renewed. The cool air picked up, and Hannah pulled her shawl tighter under her chin. And as she looked across the land spread in the valley below, it was as if she was seeing it for the first time. Where once there had been only barren fields months ago, now lay barley crops ripe for harvest—a blessing from the Almighty.

In the distance, the call of a solitary night bird sang a haunting melody. Yes, there were worries about the Philistines and idol worshipers among them, yet it was also a time of hope, like a lamp burning in a vast wilderness.

A new sense of purpose filled the space between them when they rose. Hannah whispered, "Lord, help me to trust. Help me to believe."

Elkanah stepped out first, and as Hannah followed, the olive grove served as a silent witness to their faith, their love, and the pressing times that shaped them. The moonlit path ahead seemed to glow with promise. The wind whispered again as if carrying their prayers into the night. This time the rustling leaves seemed to echo a soft "Amen."

"I will continue to pray with you," Elkanah said softly, his voice a comforting balm to her weary soul.

She nodded, unable to speak, her throat closed with emotion.

Elkanah must have sensed her sadness, because he pulled her close again as he gazed at the stars. "Do not lose heart, Hannah," he whispered. "The Lord sees your faithfulness. He hears your prayers."

Tears filled her eyes as she leaned into his strength. "I know, Elkanah. I trust in His plan." The words slipped out easily. Hannah hoped she truly believed them.

CHAPTER NINE

The sun lifted over the horizon as Hannah looked out at her family, gathered to begin their journey to Shiloh. Elkanah needed no map for the well-trodden path from Ramathaim to Shiloh. He had walked the same path since he was a child.

Children with rumpled hair and sleepy faces stumbled around, yet excitement sparkled in their eyes. Even though the journey would take two days, there was a feeling of celebration. It was *Pesach*, or Passover, a time to commemorate the liberation of the Israelites from Egyptian bondage.

The dry wind tugged at Hannah's head covering. Elkanah fussed with the bags. Peninnah organized her children, and Hannah glanced down at her empty arms. Last night's prayers had brought a balm to her soul, yet an ache remained.

Elkanah inspected the oxcart, ensuring everything was securely fastened. His words carried through the early morning air as he spoke to one of the servants, a note of satisfaction in his tone. Hannah's heart swelled with affection and gratitude for her husband. He would lead their family's procession, his strong voice guiding them in prayer, his eyes watchful for any potential danger on the road.

Peninnah was nearby, her weary face softened by the morning light as she tended to the children. She looked up and caught Hannah's eye. New anger stirred in her expression—an anger Hannah didn't understand.

"Are we ready?" Elkanah called to Hannah.

"I believe so," Hannah replied.

"Good," Elkanah said. "Let us begin."

The family began to move, and the oxcart, loaded with offerings and supplies, creaked. Elkanah walked at the head of the group, setting a steady pace. Peninnah was with the children, her voice rising and falling as she called instructions and admonitions to them. Hannah brought up the rear, walking among the servants.

Hannah found her gaze drawn to the sky, and she resisted the urge to look over her shoulder and glance at the watchtower. Last night's tender moment with Elkanah almost seemed like a dream.

The road ahead was crowded with neighboring families, all traveling together in a shared pilgrimage. From the valley below, the voices of men and women lifted in conversation and excitement.

Hannah's thoughts lingered on Peninnah's angry expression. Was it because she had witnessed the tender moments between Elkanah and Hannah over the past few days? Hannah guessed so, but she couldn't shake the feeling that something else was amiss.

As she walked, Hannah discovered a newfound empathy for the younger woman. They were on this journey together, not just to Shiloh but through the complexities of their shared life. It was a path of challenges and joys, lessons and faith, and a profound connection to a heritage that had endured for generations.

Elkanah, who must have dropped back to the rear of their group while she was lost in thought, reached out to take her hand, his touch a reassuring warmth.

"Are you well, Hannah?" he asked, his gentle eyes concerned.

She smiled and nodded and watched as Peninnah left their group, youngest children napping in the cart, to join her friends for a while. She talked and laughed with them, but her laughter seemed too loud, too sharp, even across the distance between them and Hannah.

As the hours passed, their feet became dusty with the miles they traveled. The children's playful energy waned. This was only the first of three pilgrimages for the year. Next came *Shavuot*, or the Festival of Weeks, held seven weeks after Passover. It was a time of joyous celebration and thanksgiving, marking the giving of the Torah at Mount Sinai. During that holiday, the family would bring offerings of new grain, acknowledging Yahweh's blessing on their fields.

Lastly, *Sukkot*, or the Festival of Booths, was in the fall. They would dwell in temporary shelters to remember the wandering in the wilderness, a poignant reminder of their reliance on Yahweh's providence.

The journey to Shiloh was physically taxing, each step an encounter with the relentlessness of the road—a battle against the bustling chaos from neighboring tribes converging with them to undertake the same trip. Friends greeted each other, their voices carrying stories and news from their villages.

Elkanah gave her hand a tender squeeze and then strode off to join a friend in the crowd—an elder from another tribe. He waved, calling out a warm greeting. Other men soon congregated, exchanging handshakes and hearty claps on the back. They continued walking together, their voices deep and resonant as they discussed the latest harvest and shared memories of past festivals.

Eleven-year-old Zemir, Elkanah's third youngest son, slipped his hand into Hannah's. Unlike his brothers, Zemir was small for his size and frail. If anyone fell sick in their home, it was usually him. Hannah looked down and noticed streaks of tears lining his dusty face.

"What is wrong, Zemir?" Hannah asked.

"They laughed at me, *Doda* Hannah." Zemir's voice quavered. "When I fell, they all laughed."

Hannah's heart ached for the boy, and she squeezed his hand tight, offering comfort. "I know it hurts when people laugh at you," she said gently. "But you must not let their taunting affect you. Remember, you are strong and brave, just like your abba."

"Is that why you never get upset when people tease you?" Zemir's big eyes looked up at her, shining with curiosity and a hint of admiration.

Hannah smiled, touched by his perceptiveness. "Yes, Zemir. I have learned that people's words only have power if we let them. We must remember who we are and who we belong to. Yahweh made us special, and no one's laughter can take that away."

Zemir's grasp tightened around Hannah's fingers as they advanced toward a cluster of mingling women. His brown eyes flitted about, absorbing the multitude of new faces from the groups and families merging upon the road. The air vibrated with a medley of voices, each group bringing a unique accent and tone.

"Do you really believe that, Doda Hannah?" he asked.

"With all my heart," Hannah reassured him, bending down to his level. "You are wonderful just as you are. Those who truly care for you will see that. Let us not worry about those who do not understand."

Zemir wiped his tears and gave her a tentative smile. He nodded, his young face showing a newfound determination.

"It is all right, Zemir," Hannah continued. "We will meet new friends and share this special time with them. And always remember, you are loved and never alone."

Zemir's steps became more purposeful, more assured. Soon he released Hannah's hand and raced off to find the other children.

Hannah joined a few older women walking nearby and greetings and introductions with them. If the women knew her story, they gave no indication. Hannah certainly didn't feel compelled to share it, but only to enjoy the companionship.

Just ahead, Hannah spotted some of the other Levite musicians, their instruments strapped to their backs, engaged in animated discussion. It was not long before Elkanah joined them. Soon the musicians tuned their instruments and began to sing.

The dusty road to Shiloh was transformed yet again. Not just by the convergence of people but by the voices of the Levites that rose in a harmonious melody floating on the breeze. Men, women, and children joined in, their voices blending in a chorus of praise.

Hannah walked on, her steps buoyed by the music. Elkanah's voice rang out, solid and recognizable. She teared up with emotion as she looked up at the endless blue sky, her soul lifted by the music. She was part of something eternal, beautiful, and blessed.

The gentle rustle of robes drew Hannah's attention, and she turned to find an older woman approaching. Her hair was a soft silver, and lines of grace and wisdom etched her face. She bore the gentle dignity of a lifetime devoted to serving Yahweh, carrying herself with a quiet authority, familiar yet imposing. Something about the woman seemed familiar.

Recognition dawned. "Rina!" It was the wife of Levi from the next village over. "You led the women's choir when I was younger."

Rina's eyes twinkled, and she clasped Hannah's hands warmly. "Yes, dear child. I remember you too, and I lead the women's choir still. A messenger arrived yesterday asking if you could join the choir this year. Elkanah sent him."

Hannah's heart leaped. "Elkanah sent a messenger? I did not know he went to so much trouble." Yet he must have. How else could he have received word already?

Rina's laughter was rich and comforting. "Well, he did. And it was a wonderful surprise. I told him yes, of course. I assume you remember the songs? Also, I packed one of the special linen robes for you that the women wear."

Hannah's joy bubbled over, and her voice trembled with excitement. "Oh, Rina, thank you. Elkanah told me I could join the choir, but I had forgotten about the robes. I am so thrilled! How is Ruth? Will she be in the choir as well?"

Rina's face fell, and her expression clouded with sorrow and anger. "I sent Ruth with her abba to assist him and to serve at the tabernacle last year." Rina paused, her steps slowing, her eyes darting around to ensure no one else was listening. "She is of marrying age now, but that will never be."

Hannah gasped, leaning closer. "What do you mean?"

With a deep breath, Rina spoke, her voice trembling. "Ruth was so eager to serve at the tabernacle among the other daughters of the Levite workers. It was an honor—baking bread and cleaning—yet also a time of spiritual growth." Rina swallowed hard, her gaze dropping. "But she was violated by one of Eli's sons. She returned home, her spirit shattered, living every day shrouded in her shame."

Hannah's heart felt as though a blade had pierced it. She gasped and then quickly covered her mouth with her hand. "Eli's son? How could the high priest, a man of Yahweh, allow his flesh and blood to commit such an abominable act under the roof of Yahweh's sanctuary?"

Hannah's mind raced, Elkanah's words from their past conversations flooding back. Her husband had often spoken in hushed tones of the degradation of the priesthood under Eli's watch. Elkanah told her about Eli's sons, who were scoundrels without respect for the Lord or their duties as priests. They abused their power, took advantage of their position, and openly defied Yahweh instead of serving Him as they ought.

"It is not just this incident, Rina," Hannah said, her voice cracking with emotion. "Elkanah has told me other stories that paint a grim picture of the tabernacle's current state. Eli's sons are known to be wicked men, lacking in integrity and honor. They have been stealing from the offerings and mistreating those who come to worship. It is as if they have completely forgotten what it means to be a servant of Yahweh."

Rina's footsteps slowed, and Hannah matched her gait. "And yet they continue to serve? How can Eli allow this? How can he let them destroy something so sacred?"

"I do not know," Hannah admitted, feeling profoundly helpless. "I only know that we must do what we can. We must pray for change, for justice, for a return to the ways of righteousness. Our Yahweh is a God of justice and will not let wickedness go unpunished forever."

The two women walked in silence. Hannah's heart weighed like a boulder inside her. How far things had fallen. Farther than she had ever imagined. Once a beacon of spiritual nourishment and connection to Yahweh, the tabernacle had been turned into a den of corruption. She had heard these things from Elkanah. But Rina's daughter was living proof of the horrible truth.

Yet, amid the despair, she felt a spark of hope. They were not powerless. They had the weapon of prayer. Together, her people would continue petitioning Yahweh, trusting He would hear their cries and intervene to restore purity and holiness to His dwelling place.

Will you pray for such, yet not for a son?

The whisper nearly stopped Hannah in her tracks, yet just as quickly, she pushed it out of her mind. That was different. Praying for a son was personal, wasn't it?

"Whatever shall be done about this?" Hannah dared to ask.

Rina's face showed both fury and despair. Her voice was a taut thread, barely keeping her emotions in check. "The tabernacle, which should be a place of refuge and holiness, has become tainted. Many of us are losing faith in the leadership. We have begun praying earnestly that Yahweh will raise from among us a just leader. Someone who will not turn a blind eye, someone who will cleanse this corruption."

Around them, the festive mood continued, but the joy had left the two women. It felt as if a dark cloud had settled over them, casting long, cold shadows, dampening the vibrant atmosphere of the day. Hannah's eyes were wet with empathy and the weight of the news. She knew all too well the pain of a heart heavy with grief and unmet expectations.

She reached out and took Rina's trembling hand, squeezing it reassuringly. "Rina," Hannah began, with conviction in her voice, "I believe in a Yahweh who sees and knows. He watches over us and hears the cries of the oppressed. We must not lose faith. We must keep praying and keep believing. Yahweh sees Ruth and all His daughters who suffer in silence. He will not be silent forever."

CHAPTER TEN

A s the group of travelers reached a particularly steep incline, the descending sun painted the landscape in hues of gold and amber. Hannah knew the road to Shiloh well, with its twists and turns, its risings and falls, much like the Israelites' journey.

She saw Elkanah, positioned ahead with the other Levites, pause and look back at the multitude of pilgrims. The softest smile played on his lips as he surveyed the flushed faces and tired bodies but also the unbroken spirits of the assembled crowd.

Her husband's hand rose, demanding attention, his voice a powerful echo over the congregation. "Brothers and sisters, we are about to ascend this rise and descend into the valley, the final trail to Shiloh. Let us sing one of the Songs of Ascent. Let our voices rise as we climb, a physical expression of our spiritual journey."

A murmur of agreement rippled through the crowd. The Levites positioned themselves and readied their instruments.

Hannah stood among the women, her heart pulsing with a rhythm that echoed in her soul. As the notes of the Song of Ascent filled the air, something profound stirred within her. Her palms were damp, and her shallow breath quickened.

Each word of longing, hope, joy, and trust in Yahweh seemed to resonate in her core, pulling her closer to something divine, something pure.

The anticipation was not just a fleeting emotion but a physical sensation. It was as if a string was tied around her heart, tugging her toward a spiritual pinnacle even as her body moved toward the top of an earthly hill.

Elkanah led the melody as the other Levites joined harmoniously. Every verse sung was a step closer to Shiloh. The song was a journey in itself, a rising crescendo of belief.

The air was thick with emotion, the women's voices blending in harmonious unison with the men's and then the children's too. Hannah could hear each individual longing and prayer, and together they were part of something greater. A testament to the timeless faith that connected her to a past filled with the same songs. It was fitting and right, and in that moment, it was everything.

When they reached the top, Hannah paused, looking back at their path. There were more hills ahead before they reached their destination. After a night of rest, a half-day's journey would take them to Shiloh.

The sun was setting behind the mountains, painting the sky with a warm orange and pink hue. The air was crisp and refreshing, carrying the scent of pine trees and wildflowers. A gentle breeze rustled through the leaves. In the distance, a family of deer grazed peacefully in a clearing.

Elkanah led the family to a resting place where other pilgrims already gathered. A grassy area near a gentle stream offered a welcome respite for weary feet and tired animals.

Around them, other families began to set up temporary shelters, tend to livestock, and prepare modest meals over small fires. The air was heavy with the enticing aromas of cooking, mingled with the more earthy scents of the road and land around them.

Humming the Song of Ascent, Elkanah worked to set up their camp with the help of his oldest sons, Eitan and Oren. Sweat clung to their brows, and their muscles strained from the day's exertion, yet their faces were etched with smiles of satisfaction.

"Oren, make sure the stakes are driven deep. We do not want the tents to blow away in the night," Elkanah instructed, his voice steady and sure.

"I understand, Abba," Oren replied, his young hands skillfully managing the task along with his brother Eitan.

As they worked, Hannah glanced over at Abiram, Elkanah's twelve-year-old son, playing king of the stone pile with other children. A young boy with a head full of curls reached the top and stretched out his arms. "I am the king of the Philistines!" he called.

"Why king of the Philistines?" Abiram asked. "Why not king of the Israelites?"

Abiram suddenly stopped and looked up at his abba, curious. "Abba, why don't we have a king like the other nations? Why are we different?"

Elkanah knelt beside his son, his face gentle. "We are different, Abiram, because Yahweh is our king. He guides, protects, and loves us more than any earthly king could. He is always with us, even when we cannot see Him."

Abiram looked thoughtful. "So, Yahweh is with us now? On this journey?"

"Yes, my son," Elkanah affirmed, his voice strong with conviction. "Yahweh is here in the songs, our hearts, and the air we breathe. He is what makes this journey sacred."

With the camp finally set up, Hannah found a comfortable spot near the fire and settled down with a sigh of contentment. Elkanah joined her, his face glowing from exertion, the warmth of the flames, and the joy of the day. The songs accompanying them on the road continued to fill the air.

"I have never heard such beautiful singing." Hannah looked up at the star-filled sky. "It is as if the heavens have joined us in our praise."

Elkanah smiled and squeezed her hand. "And it will continue. These songs are the heartbeat of our faith."

From a nearby camp, a group of young Levites began a new song. Their voices rose. Other voices joined in, creating a chorus that encompassed all of creation.

Hannah leaned against Elkanah's shoulder, listening to the interwoven voices, feeling the vibrations of the song in her soul. Even Peninnah, who was settling the younger children for the night, hummed with a smile on her lips. Their rivalry seemed more distant now. Perhaps Hannah needed only to give their relationship time to grow into one of mutual respect.

The echoes of the traditional songs faded, and a hushed silence fell upon the encampment. It was then that Elkanah stood. Hannah expected him to move into his tent for the night. Instead, standing tall, Elkanah looked out over the other tents. Then he began to sing. His strong voice rang out in the cool night air. "I lift my eyes to the mountains—where does my help come from? My help comes from the Lord, the Maker of heaven and earth."

His words were haunting and powerful. Soon others joined in—from within the tents and under the night sky—their voices rising in a crescendo of faith and longing.

"He will not let your foot slip; He who watches over you will not slumber."

Hannah listened, tears forming in her eyes. The words spoke to her deepest fears and hopes. Elkanah's features were illuminated by the flickering firelight.

"Behold, how good and pleasant it is when brothers dwell in unity! The Lord watches over you—the Lord is your shade at your right hand. The sun will not harm you by day, nor the moon by night."

Around them, other families joined in, the music swelling and filling the night.

The song ended, leaving a resonant silence in the air, filled with emotion and connection.

Standing tall among the Levite musicians, Elkanah was not finished. He cleared his throat and began to sing again, a melody seemingly birthed in the moment. Her husband's words flowed unbidden. She felt every note, every word.

From the valleys we arise, our voices joined as one,
On the road to Shiloh, under the rising sun.
With hearts of faith and hands of grace, we seek the
    sacred way;
Together on this journey, in unity we'll stay.

The other Levites picked up the melody, their instruments beautifully blending and supporting Elkanah's voice.

Hannah stood and felt a thrill at the new song. It spoke directly to their experience, capturing the essence of their journey in a way that was both timeless and immediate. She joined the chorus, her voice strong and clear.

Behold, how sweet the path we tread, with brothers,
    sisters dear;
The way to Shiloh's hallowed ground, where Yahweh's
    voice we'll hear.
We'll offer thanks and sing His praise; in harmony we'll
    stand,
United in His love and grace as we reach the promised
    land.

Suddenly, Hannah's ears caught another voice, distant but growing stronger, one she would know anywhere. It was Ayala's. Hannah saw she was approaching with her husband and a few straggling travelers. Concern filled Simeon's face. He appeared worn from the journey yet alert to the needs of his young wife. Elkanah turned, noticing them too. He sang one more line then let the song fade away.

Hannah felt the urge to run to check on Ayala, but she knew it was not her place. Her heart ached with the desire to be near, to help, but she remained still. Peninnah went to her daughter, and even in the twilight, Hannah could tell that Ayala was putting on a good show, masking her fatigue with a smile.

Elkanah stepped before Hannah, his eyes kind yet firm. "She has her own family now," he said, his tone gentle but unwavering. "Ayala and Simeon will set up their tent with Peninnah's help, and they will be fine, I promise."

Hannah's heart still throbbed with worry, but she had no choice but to trust Elkanah's judgment. *It is not your place,* she told herself again.

The night was quiet now, the songs replaced by the gentle rustling of the wind and the distant cries of night creatures. Crawling into her tent alone then settling herself, Hannah tried to pray. She couldn't. Not yet. The day had been beautiful, the songs touched her heart, but deep down, she still questioned. Did Yahweh hear her? Did He care?

Hannah thought of Elkanah's words to Abiram. *"Yahweh is here in the songs, our hearts, and the air we breathe. He is what makes this journey sacred."* Hannah knew this with her mind, but year after year of unanswered prayers had sealed up her heart, though she continued to feel it opening.

"Yahweh, I want to pray. I want to believe. Stir my heart the way the wind stirs the night." The whispered words slipped from Hannah's lips as she fell asleep with Elkanah's songs playing in her memory.

CHAPTER ELEVEN

Hannah's hands worked deftly, flipping flatbreads over the crackling fire. The early-morning sun filtered through the leaves, casting dappled shadows on the ground. The scent of spices mingled with the smoky smell of the firewood. The gentle sizzle of the cooking food was a comforting sound, grounding her in this new day—their last day before reaching Shiloh.

But in an instant, everything changed. A figure burst from the woods near the edge of the road. Hannah immediately recognized Elkanah's oldest son. The same boy who wielded a wooden sword in play fighting now ran without a glance over his shoulder. His face was pale.

"Eitan!" Hannah exclaimed as the young teen came running toward her. "What is wrong?"

"Doda Hannah," he panted, his voice trembling, "something is wrong with Ayala. I saw her slip into the wooded area near the road. She was crying. Something is wrong."

Hannah's heart leaped into her throat, terror clutching at her chest. She dropped the cooking utensil and wiped her hands on her apron, her mind racing. She took a deep breath. It would do no good to panic.

"What do you mean, Eitan? What happened?"

"I do not know," Eitan cried, tears welling in his eyes. "She looked scared. She would not talk to me. She just covered her mouth and hurried away."

Without another word, Hannah's feet were moving, carrying her toward the treed area. The taste of flatbread that lingered in her mouth turned bitter.

As she rushed into the woods, Eitan behind her, branches whipped at her face. From back at the campsite, her ears caught the faint sound of a voice calling her name. *Elkanah? Is that Elkanah calling me?* She couldn't be sure. Her heartbeat pounded in her ears, drowning out everything else.

The underbrush was dense and the ground uneven, and Hannah's breath came in ragged gasps as she plunged deeper into the forest. Every rustle of leaves, every snapped twig, heightened her anxiety.

Where is Ayala? What had happened to her?

Questions swirled in Hannah's mind, each one amplifying her fear, sharpening her senses. The woods seemed to close around her, the shadows growing darker, the silence more profound.

"Eitan, stay close!" she called over her shoulder. Not daring to look back, her eyes strained to see through the gloom.

But Eitan's voice was also lost to her now. All that remained was the chilling silence of the woods and the haunting possibility that she had heard Elkanah's voice telling her to stop. Did he know something?

Hannah's eyes searched the woods. She thought of the day Ayala had followed her a decade ago. The day the Philistines attacked. One hour later and they would have both been killed or captured. A shiver ran up her spine.

The suspense was unbearable, the tension a living thing that gripped her very soul.

Hannah stumbled over unseen roots and rocks, her breath rasping in her throat as she plunged deeper into the gloom of the woods. The sun rose, casting the world in a dim, uncertain light, and the woods seemed to shift and sway around her as though concealing secrets.

"Ayala!" Hannah tripped, falling to the ground, her hands scraping against the rough earth. Pain shot up her arm, but she scarcely noticed it. Panic and confusion clouded her mind, and questions tumbled through her thoughts.

Why had Eitan come to *her*? Why hadn't he run to Simeon or Peninnah? Was it a mistake not to tell Elkanah that Ayala had disappeared into the woods?

She scrambled back to her feet, her chest tight with fear. Where was Peninnah? Hannah had spent so much time with Ayala over the years, nurturing her, loving her as if she were her own daughter. Ayala was her constant companion, joining her as she baked and cooked, a bright spot in her life.

Hannah's mind spun with fear and anger. Anger at Peninnah for her neglect, anger at herself for not knowing what to do, anger at the world for the unfairness of it all. Anger at Yahweh for not giving her these children. Why not her?

She pressed on, her body aching, her mind racing. The woods seemed to close around her, the trees whispering secrets she couldn't hear, the shadows hiding dangers she couldn't see.

"Ayala!"

With every step, the tension grew. Hannah's senses sharpened, attuned to every rustle of leaves, every snap of a twig. The woods were quiet, and the shadows deep.

Suddenly, a figure came into view, leaning against a tree, her face pale and eyes wide with shock.

"Ayala!" Hannah cried, rushing up to her. Her heart pounded with relief and concern. "What are you doing here? What is wrong?"

The sound of footsteps became more evident as Hannah stilled. Eitan, trailing behind her, caught up and said to Ayala, "I saw you crying, and you looked sick. I did not know what to do, so I went to find Hannah."

Ayala's face went pale. Her eyes darted between Hannah and Eitan. "I will be fine," she insisted, her voice wavering. "I just need a moment." She wiped at her mouth with the back of her hand.

Eitan, unable to contain his concern, pressed his fists to his hips. "You are not fine," he said, his voice cracking.

Ayala turned to Hannah, her eyes pleading. "Can we talk alone, please?"

Hannah nodded and motioned for Eitan to return to their camp, reassuring him everything would be okay.

Once alone, Ayala looked away. Her hands trembled. Before she could speak, something in her expression—in the tears welling in her eyes—struck a chord deep within Hannah. A realization hit her, as clear and startling as a bolt of lightning.

"You are expecting a child," Hannah whispered, her voice holding a knowing that transcended mere guesswork.

Ayala nodded, fresh tears spilling down her cheeks. "Yes," she choked out, "but I did not want to hurt you. Sickness in the morning overwhelms me these days, and I knew you would recognize what my sickness really was. So I came here and tried to hide it. I know how much you have wanted a child."

A complex whirl of emotions filled Hannah. There was certainly joy for Ayala but also a pang of sorrow, a reminder of her unfulfilled longing. Yet as she looked into Ayala's eyes, she saw not just the fear of hurting her but also the radiant glow of new life, a beautiful and sacred miracle.

"You have not hurt me, Ayala." Hannah's voice was steady, and her heart overflowed with genuine happiness. "This is a joyous occasion. One I was sure would happen for you. We must celebrate it."

Ayala's face softened, and Hannah saw the relief washing over her. "But how can you be so selfless? How can you not feel the pain?"

Hannah took Ayala's hands, hoping her touch was warm and comforting. "Of course a part of me feels the ache of my desires, but that does not diminish the beauty of what is happening in your life. Our faith teaches us to rejoice in blessings and trust Yahweh's plan. Your child is a part of that plan."

"Are you sure?" Ayala rubbed her brow.

"Sure?" Hannah laughed. "This is a blessing, a beautiful new beginning for you and Simeon."

Ayala's eyes filled with tears as she looked at Hannah, her vulnerability laid bare. "But what if I am not ready? What if I cannot be the imma my child needs?"

Hannah embraced Ayala, her heart aching for the young woman's uncertainty and fear. "You will be a wonderful imma, Ayala. You have a heart full of love, which is the most important thing a child needs."

Ayala's tears subsided, and she looked up at Hannah with deep gratitude. "Thank you, Hannah. What would I do without you?"

Hannah smiled. Unshed tears misted her eyes, and she blinked them back. "You will never have to find out. We will face this new future together. Now let us return."

When they reached the clearing, Hannah paused. Ayala did the same.

"I just have to ask one thing." Hannah offered what she hoped was a gentle smile.

Ayala adjusted her shawl. "Yes?"

"Does your abba know?" Hannah's voice wavered.

Ayala locked gazes with Hannah. "Simeon told Abba last night. Abba said he would tell you today as we walked along the road."

"Does everyone consider me so frail?" New tears sprang to Hannah's eyes—pain that those she loved would have to feel guilty to be given such a great gift as a child.

"I…I did not want to add to your pain, dear Hannah," Ayala admitted. "Abba was worried too. It is indeed a joyous occasion for my imma. She will be a grandmother now, but I understand the sting it provokes in your heart."

Hannah sighed. "I only ask that you allow me to hold your child. To love him. To tickle his toes…" Hannah tilted her head and peered at the young woman. "Can you allow me to do that without worries about what anyone thinks?"

Ayala clasped her hands in front of her. "Yes, of course!"

"Then I have only good things to look forward to." Hannah's laughter broke through the morning air. She pulled Ayala into another hug. "Oh, Ayala, this is wonderful news! Truly wonderful!"

Ayala's face lit up at Hannah's reaction, the worry and uncertainty melting away under the warmth of Hannah's joy. "You mean that?" Ayala asked, a tentative smile on her lips.

"Of course I do." Hannah again took Ayala's hands on her own. "I could not be happier for you and Simeon."

Hannah led Ayala back to her campsite with a newfound lightness in her steps. Then she helped Ayala wash up.

Her heart thumped with anticipation. Previously she ached with each friend's announced pregnancy—even more so when it was Peninnah's—but this was different. This was Ayala, her dear Ayala, and the news brought nothing but joy.

Their heartfelt moment was interrupted by the sound of approaching footsteps. Hannah turned. Elkanah walked toward her, Simeon at his side. Their brows were furrowed with concern.

Elkanah's attention fixed on Hannah—his expression full of anticipation and uncertainty. "I was going to tell you," he began.

Hannah's heart skipped a beat, and she looked from Elkanah to Ayala. "You already knew, Husband, yet you kept the news to yourself." She lifted one eyebrow and waited, even though she knew the answer.

Elkanah nodded, his expression full of compassion. "Yes, Simeon told me earlier. I wanted to find the right moment to share the news with you."

Standing a bit apart, Simeon looked on. His face reflected his complex emotions. He was a new husband and soon-to-be abba, but Hannah could tell these were not the types of conversations he was used to being a part of.

Hannah touched Elkanah's arm. "It is all right. I know, and I am truly happy for them."

Elkanah's shoulders relaxed, and he returned her smile, the connection between them as strong and supportive as ever. "I knew you would understand, but I was still worried. Your heart has been heavy for so long."

"I know," Hannah whispered, her eyes shimmering with unshed tears. "But today, we celebrate Ayala and Simeon's blessing. We rejoice in the promise of new life."

Together, they turned back toward the camp. When they approached the tent, Hannah saw that Peninnah was talking to Eitan. Peninnah's face was drawn, and her eyes seemed clouded with something Hannah couldn't quite place. Was she upset because Eitan sought out Hannah instead of her in his fear for Ayala?

New compassion for Peninnah grew within Hannah, continuing to soften the edges of old grievances and misunderstandings. Without a word, she left Elkanah's side and went to help Peninnah pack up.

Peninnah looked up, startled by Hannah's presence, but said nothing. Still, Hannah could feel her deep sadness.

The two women worked together, the unspoken understanding growing as they prepared for the remaining journey ahead. Today, they would be in Shiloh. And today, one of Hannah's greatest pains had turned into great joy. Would there be more transformations in the week to come?

A few hours later, as they set out on the road, the echoes of yesterday's songs filled the air. Something was different about this pilgrimage. Hannah already felt it deep inside.

CHAPTER TWELVE

A s Hannah's family approached the sacred ground of
Shiloh in the gentle warmth of spring, their path led
them through the vineyards that bordered the holy city. The
landscape had shifted from arid plains, giving way to lush, rolling hills. The scent in the air was fresh and invigorating.

The vineyards were a sight to behold, a living tapestry of
green interwoven with the rich earth. Row upon row of grapevines stretched toward the horizon, their leaves just beginning
to bud. The vines were laden with the promise of future fruit,
the clusters still in their infancy, waiting for the sun's kiss to
ripen them into deep shades of purple and red.

In the fields, the vineyard workers moved with practiced
grace. Their hands deftly tended to the vines, pruning and
guiding them to flourish. The gentle young leaves danced in
the wind, accompanied by the occasional birdcall or the vineyard workers' soft conversation.

For Hannah, the beauty of the vineyards was a reflection of
the Creator's wisdom and grace, a tangible symbol of Yahweh's
faithfulness to His people.

Peninnah walked behind the rest of the family, talking
with the other women. She kept her distance again today. Ayala
walked ahead with Simeon's imma and sisters instead of

walking with her own imma. From their excited voices and laughter, Hannah guessed that Ayala had told them all the joyous news of their expanding family.

Even though pain attempted to pull her back, new hope pushed Hannah forward. The tranquility of the scene calmed her soul and fortified her spirit. Amid these vineyards, she felt a profound connection to her faith and a renewed sense of purpose. The simple, natural beauty around her was a reminder that Yahweh's presence was everywhere.

Hannah's thoughts drifted again to Ayala's recent announcement. The news of her pregnancy was a cause for celebration— a new branch in the family tree, a new life that would soon bloom. Yet Hannah also battled the pang of sadness that tried to spring up within her.

Yahweh, help ease my heart.

Hannah looked at the vine keepers as they worked to carefully prune the unproductive plants. They were masters of their craft, knowing precisely what to cut and what to leave, guiding the vines to reach their fullest potential. Their actions were a combination of care and understanding, a relationship forged through the years.

She must do the same with her feelings. She must be the vine keeper of her soul, carefully pruning away the unproductive emotions that threatened to choke the joy she felt for Ayala and her growing family. She must nurture the positive feelings, allowing them to flourish and fill her heart.

With a newfound determination, Hannah quickened her steps and pushed down the sadness, focusing instead on the happiness she felt for Ayala. Ayala's child would be loved and cherished, a precious addition to their family. Hannah would be there for them, offering support, wisdom, and unconditional love.

As the sojourners continued on their path, the silhouette of the tabernacle began to emerge in the distance. With a heart full of gratitude and her eyes fixed on the sacred site, Hannah pressed onward, thinking of the celebration.

From up ahead, Elkanah slowed his steps. He fell in stride beside her and pointed.

She smiled. "Almost there."

"Yes, and I am excited about that. Something is different this year." Elkanah chuckled. "I feel it, don't you?"

She glanced up at her husband and offered a playful smile. "Hope?"

"Maybe." Elkanah winked and reached out to touch a leaf. "I like the sound of that."

Hannah followed suit, feeling a grape leaf's cool, smooth skin between her fingers, marveling at the life within. The vine seemed to breathe beneath her touch.

Elkanah began to hum a familiar tune, and Hannah knew that his voice would rise in song as soon as they reached the city gates. Even though Elkanah enjoyed singing among the other Levite singers and musicians along the way, it had become a tradition for him to seek out Hannah so they could walk into the city together. Sometimes, Hannah sang along, her voice harmonizing with his. Other times she would just listen, her soul absorbing the rich timbre of his voice and the warmth of his devotion. But always, her heart would expand with pride to be at her husband's side.

Peninnah's voice rose sharply behind them as she reprimanded one of her children. Her words were harsher than usual, with an uncharacteristic edge that made fellow travelers turn to gawk. Elkanah's steps slowed, and his shoulders tensed.

Hannah glanced over and offered him a quick nod. Her eyes met his, conveying understanding and reassurance. "I will be fine," she said. "I see Simeon up ahead under that cluster of trees. I imagine Ayala is resting. Do what you must to help Peninnah, and I will take a moment and join your daughter." Hannah smiled. "Do not worry, my husband. I will wait to enter Shiloh with you."

Without a word, Elkanah walked back toward his second wife and his children. His silhouette receded into the distance, but Hannah's gaze lingered on him, gratitude welling within her for the man he was.

For twenty years she had walked this road as a wife. Was there even a time before she was Elkanah's bride? It was hard to remember.

As she continued on, her thoughts wandered back to their early days, to the young love that blossomed into a deep and enduring connection. She remembered their first pilgrimage together and the nervous excitement she felt. They were full of the promise of life ahead. Through the years, there had been trials, tears, and laughter. Hannah looked forward, once again, to their reunion at the city's gates.

The familiar sights and scents on the roadway also triggered a flood of recollections of her childhood—a vivid image of her past. Growing up, she played in fields similar to these vineyards. She chased the songbirds until her legs grew weary. Then she would find one of her uncles and beg for tales of heroes and faith.

Among those stories, she loved the story of Samson best. Perhaps because she could still remember when a messenger arrived sharing Samson's accomplishment of defeating thousands of their enemies in a single day. God had set Samson apart and endowed him with supernatural strength. Yet he was flawed and human. He made wrong choices, and life did not go perfectly for him. In a way, that gave Hannah hope.

As she neared the tree where a small gathering of their clan rested, Hannah considered how Samson's life was intertwined with the vineyards. He was forbidden to touch the fruit of the vine as part of his Nazarite vow. The vineyards symbolized temptation and the need for restraint for him, a daily reminder of his covenant with God. Samson's whole life could be summed up in his battle between his spiritual calling and his earthly desires.

Just as Samson struggled with his weaknesses, Hannah had internal battles too. Her longing for a child was a constant ache, a desire that sometimes threatened to overshadow her faith and contentment.

She considered Samson's ultimate redemption, his final act of faith that brought him back to God. His sacrifice. Samson gave his life—all that he had.

Samson gave it all. No matter what people said about his wrong choices, Samson chose well in the end.

Dust, kicked up from fellow travelers, tickled her nose, and Hannah pulled her shawl tighter around herself. Her thoughts bounced to other ancestors her people now revered. *"The call of God gives much and requires much,"* her abba had often said. Maybe it was better Yahweh hadn't answered her prayer. Perhaps she was not strong enough for a greater calling than to be a wife.

Even as Elkanah watched his sons in mock battle back at home, she often saw a deeper concern in his gaze. Their play with wooden swords was amusing until one understood that someday it wouldn't be play. The danger of the Philistines was ever present.

Peninnah had five sons given to her, and yet she also had five sons she could lose. Hannah's heart squeezed. *Maybe the Lord knows what I can handle. Maybe He sees I am not strong enough to face the possibility of losing a son.*

The words wove through Hannah's mind as she moved off the downtrodden pathway, stepping through the taller grasses toward the trees, where she spotted a large family group. Ayala was sitting with them. *Then again, I will never know.*

Hannah pushed down the sadness that threatened to overwhelm her, thinking once again of the vine keepers cutting away the unproductive vines. She approached Ayala, who rested under a cluster of trees, her face flushed with fatigue and with the glow of new life within her. Simeon was at her side, tenderly supporting her.

Ayala's face looked pale, and Hannah guessed that she couldn't keep anything down. Hannah pressed her fingers to her lips as worry sprouted up like weeds in her mind. She did not want to think about the half-dozen family members and friends who had lost their lives during pregnancy or during birth.

The dozen women who also rested near Ayala turned toward her in unison, as if one had warned the others of Hannah's approach. Gazes narrowed as she reached the group. These were familiar women—some of Peninnah's sisters and cousins. Hannah could almost hear their thoughts. *Hannah, are you walking alone? And, look, your husband does not seem to care that you have to walk alone.*

Children sat around the women, from infants to older boys and girls. Each child was a silent reminder of Hannah's barrenness.

"What a great blessing that you are as fruitful as your imma," one of Ayala's older cousins declared, talking to Ayala louder than she needed to, obviously for Hannah's benefit.

Without hesitation, Simeon rushed to Hannah's side. He stood the same height as Hannah, and his warm eyes fixed on hers. "Ayala was hoping she would see you today. We have cool water and bread. Also, my wife packed some figs. She knows they are your favorite."

Hannah was about to decline, but Simeon gently clutched her elbow and led her to Ayala's side, where a blanket had already been spread. Hannah settled next to the young woman. "I do not want to interrupt."

"It is no interruption." Ayala pointed to the group members who were gathering their things. "My family is leaving. They have already been resting a while. Simeon and I arrived minutes before you approached." The young woman placed her hand on Hannah's. "Please stay," she urged.

Hannah nodded, and as the group headed out with their children, her shoulders relaxed.

Simeon blew a breath of relief as the last straggler made it onto the road. "I do love you, Ayala, but your imma's family members are so dramatic. Some love each other, and others hate each other. And then the next day it switches."

Ayala offered a soft, humored laugh. "That is because my imma was raised in a house of mostly girls."

Simeon smirked, wrapping an arm around Ayala's shoulders and pulling her close. "Well, I must admit I have always loved your stories. Your grandparents' house might have been full of drama, but from what you have told me, your own home overflowed with tales of faith and much teaching in Yahweh's laws."

Hannah wondered if Ayala would bring up Peninnah's moodiness or taunting.

Instead, Ayala, her eyes distant, leaned against her husband's shoulder, perhaps lost in the memories of her upbringing. "My abba and Hannah made sure we knew the tales of our ancestors. That we understood the struggles and the blessings. They believe the stories shape our identity as a family and a people." She paused, looking at Simeon with a playful glint in her eyes. "Perhaps if your household were filled with tales of these strong-willed Hebrew women, you would listen to me more often."

Simeon chuckled. "Maybe so. But every family has its traditions. And I love the uniqueness of both our homes."

Hannah nodded in agreement. "Indeed, the stories of our ancestors, like that of Samson, are not mere tales of the past. They are vessels of timeless and universal wisdom, carrying lessons meant to touch our hearts and shape our lives. They inspire us to live purposefully and walk paths of righteousness. They speak to the heart, not just the mind."

"You know, Hannah, there is a part of Samson's story that makes me think of you," Ayala said, her eyes full of kindness. "It is about Samson's imma. She was barren but was visited by an angel. The angel proclaimed that she would bear a son and that he would be a Nazirite, dedicated to God."

A viselike pressure built in Hannah's chest. Each heartbeat echoed the ever-raw pain of her barrenness. She felt Ayala's watchful gaze, the young woman who had seen, perhaps more than anyone else, the rise and fall of Hannah's emotions over the years.

Simeon's voice pulled Hannah from her thoughts. "What exactly is a Nazirite? My abba never truly explored the Hebrew Scriptures."

Hannah drew a deep breath before replying, "A Nazirite embraces a sacred vow—to shun unclean foods, wine, and potent drinks, to never touch the dead, and to let no razor touch one's head. It is a profound commitment to live a life consecrated to God."

"We had relatives who shared stories of such people, but Abba believed words could not stave off hunger." As Simeon spoke, he looked tenderly at his wife. "But with Ayala by my side, I have realized that wisdom feeds the spirit, and labor fills our plates. To be successful in life, and to build a strong family, we need both."

Hannah nodded, letting Simeon's words sink in. "Among our people, some simply lack knowledge and, unknowingly, commit sins of omission," she responded. As she thought of her own experiences and the many people she had encountered, an image of Eli's sons, Hophni and Phinehas, flashed in her mind. Her throat tightened with sadness. "However, there are others who should know better."

She thought of the countless times she witnessed the behavior of Eli's sons at the temple, their flagrant disregard for the sacred rituals, and the disrespect shown to those who came to worship.

"Sadly, our high priests have walked away from Yahweh's ways. Despite being raised in the shadow of the tabernacle, having the privilege of the priesthood, and being entrusted with holy duties, they are choosing a path of corruption," she mused. "Eli raised them with Yahweh's teachings. They should have felt His presence in the tabernacle, and they were surrounded by His blessings. Yet they act as if there is no Yahweh, no law."

She sighed, a heavy weight settling on her heart. "Knowing Yahweh is one thing," she murmured, "but living in His ways, respecting His teachings, and honoring His presence is entirely another."

"Our family is one that should know more, but we do not." Simeon lowered his head as if studying the blade of grass he held in his hand.

Hannah was surprised by Simeon's admission, even though she knew that generations of Israelites had lost knowledge of Yahweh because fathers had not passed down His laws to their sons.

Peninnah still did not fully approve of him. When first meeting Simeon, Elkanah had worried that Ayala's husband would not be able to lead her in the ways of the Lord. Yet as he continued to engage with the young man, Elkanah saw a tender heart and a mind willing to learn. The fact that he asked questions so openly and waited to hear the answers showed great promise.

Simeon lifted his head and rubbed his brow. "How did Samson's imma know the message was true? How did she have faith in the angel's words?" He looked from Hannah to Ayala.

Even though Ayala locked eyes with Simeon, she reached out and took Hannah's hand in her own. "She believed because she knew that Yahweh had a purpose for her, just as He has a purpose for all of us." Ayala paused as if wanting to say more.

Hannah looked up, and her gaze met Ayala's. Joy filled Ayala's face, as if she knew something Hannah did not. Something wonderful.

In that moment, Hannah felt a spark of hope ignite within her. The story of Samson's imma was not just a tale to tell one's children. It was for her. It was a promise, a reminder that Yahweh's plan was unfolding, even in her barrenness.

The tension in the air was palpable as they sat in silence, each lost in thought, the weight of history and expectation pressing down on them.

Hannah nodded. "A purpose for all of us. Indeed. It reminds us that sometimes, in our waiting and our desperation, Yahweh is preparing something beyond our wildest imaginations."

The vineyards the path led them through were a testament to patience and care, reflecting their journeys. And now, somehow, she saw those stories of the past in a new light. They became a mirror to her soul, a challenge and a comfort.

"Have faith, dear Hannah. Your time will come, and your sorrow will be turned to joy." Ayala's voice was such a soft whisper that Hannah wasn't sure if she heard it.

As Hannah considered Ayala's words, Simeon turned his gaze to the horizon. "Our journeys are filled with uncertainties, but Yahweh's love and His plans for us remain constant." One cheek lifted in a half smile. "And we should get going." Taking Ayala's hands, Simeon helped Ayala to her feet.

As they walked, Ayala wove tales of Sarah, Rebecca, and even Samson, each story rich with lessons and hope. From the questions Simeon asked, it was clear he had heard them before. Yet Ayala did not mind. She told the stories as if her husband was hearing them for the first time.

Chills ran down Hannah's arms as Ayala recited the angel's proclamation to Samson's imma, the Nazarite vow, and the purpose of the consecration.

A spark of understanding was ignited in Hannah's heart as she listened to Ayala say, "Now, knowing that next year I will have a child, bringing him or her on this journey, I think of these stories differently. None of these immas knew the stories of their children and their place in Yahweh's plan."

Hannah's thoughts wandered to her waiting, to the emptiness that haunted and shaped her. She considered the Nazarite vow, the dedication and sacrifice it symbolized, and the required faith.

As they walked, Hannah connected the threads of the stories with her own life. She felt a pull, a calling perhaps, to something greater. Yes, the Nazarite vow, a symbol of dedication and sacrifice, resonated with her deeply.

"Doesn't it seem strange that so many of our great leaders were born after years of their immas' infertility? Sarah waited, and Rachel waited. It is as if Yahweh draws their immas' hearts close first," Hannah mused, filled with wonder and longing. "Praying, dedicated immas. Yes, every great leader needs one of those."

They walked silently, the weight of history and expectation settling around them. The vineyards whispered their secrets, the fragrance of earth and green leaves filling the air, a reminder of life's cycles, of pruning and harvest.

Hannah's thoughts were joined once again by the whispered stories of Samson's imma and her vow to the Lord. A new vigor flowed through Hannah's veins, an energy birthed from understanding and purpose, transcending her yearnings.

The crowds around them swelled, the hum of conversations merging into a unified buzz of excitement. The distant silhouette of the tabernacle beckoned her. As the path they trod became more crowded, there was an undeniable certainty blooming within Hannah. This journey had evolved in ways she had not anticipated, and every step she took felt divinely orchestrated.

She could feel the rhythm of a sacred song pulsating in her heart.

I lift my eyes to the hills,
From whence does my help come?
My help comes from the Lord,
Who made heaven and earth.
He will not let your foot be moved;
He who keeps you will not slumber.

The hymn resonated deeply within her, amplifying her resolve. Her spirit soared with every verse, guiding her toward an unknown destiny.

Hannah glanced at Peninnah's children, walking ahead of her. Then she looked to Elkanah, her loving husband, and felt a surge of determination. She would pray with all her heart in Shiloh, surrounded by faith and love. She would ask the Lord for the blessing she deeply desired, trusting that He would hear her cry.

Finally, they entered the gates of Shiloh.

Each family moved to the area where they would camp. Since Elkanah was one of the Levites, Hannah and her family would press on to the center, where his kin had set up their tents for generations.

Yet as they moved closer, Hannah sensed something was wrong. There was a different feeling in the air—an unsettled aura among the sojourners. The unknown music carried on the wind diverged from the steady melodies of the songs of ascent that typically resonated around the city.

Hannah's steps slowed, gripped by unease. A nearby commotion caught her attention, but before she could identify the source, she felt a comforting hand on her shoulder. Turning, she found Elkanah beside her, his brow furrowed with concern.

Together, they approached the scene, and a knot of revulsion formed in Hannah's stomach. Scattered among the vineyards were clusters of people, their intoxication evident. Their laughter was grotesque and loud, their movements erratic and passionate. Instead of the sacred hymns of their faith, they were chanting crude words to unfamiliar tunes, their voices creating a cacophony that chilled her.

People danced around crude statues, poured libations, and offered incense. Draped in strange garb, men and women were engaging in prostrating rituals before these idols. The sight of their faces, flushed from the excess of wine and unchecked revelry, only deepened her horror of the twisted acts of devotion she was witnessing.

Hannah's heart clenched with shock. This was a stark deviation from the pure worship she knew. *How can they do such things on holy days? How can they turn their backs on Yahweh, the One who delivered them?*

Elkanah moved closer to steady her, his face mirroring her dismay.

"They have lost their way," he said softly, his voice filled with sorrow. "They have forgotten the covenant, forgotten the teachings of our ancestors."

But Hannah could not tear her eyes away from the scene. It was like a veil lifted, revealing a darkness she did not want to see.

"I do not understand," she whispered, her voice trembling. "How can they betray their faith so easily?"

Elkanah's grip tightened on her hand reassuringly. "They have been tempted by the world and its fleeting pleasures. But we must not lose hope, Hannah. We must remain steadfast. We will keep our eyes fixed on Yahweh, and we will pray for their return."

His words were a balm to her troubled soul, but the images remained, a stark reminder of the fragility of faith and the ease with which it could be lost. The vineyards, once a symbol of nature's grace and divine wisdom, now seemed tainted, their beauty marred by human folly.

With a heavy heart, Hannah turned away, focusing again on the tabernacle's silhouette, the sacred place where she would lay her burdens before the Lord.

CHAPTER THIRTEEN

A s dawn's first light painted the horizon, Hannah imagined from her dwelling how Elkanah began his day. The sky, a canvas of blush pinks and molten gold, heralded the start of a day devoted to the Lord's work.

Elkanah always initiated his duties with the essential act of purification. As he approached the laver, Hannah imagined the ritual cleansing, a bridge between the earthly and divine, an act intertwining physical purity with spiritual sanctity.

He then donned his priestly attire—the crisp linen turban, tunic, sash, and breeches, each garment a symbol of his holy dedication. She often found herself marveling at the grace and purpose with which he wore them, every fold and stitch bearing the weight of tradition and devotion.

Elkanah's first sacred task took him to the menorah, that magnificent seven-branched lampstand that stood as an eternal testament in the holy place. In her mind's eye she could see him replenishing its bowls with the finest olive oil. He trimmed its wicks, ensuring that its sacred flame flickered ceaselessly, illuminating both the tangible room and the intangible spirit. Hannah's heart swelled with pride and love, grateful for the man who honored Yahweh with such dedication.

Hannah didn't go inside the tent, of course, but Elkanah had described it and his rituals to her numerous times. She closed her eyes and pictured him moving gracefully to the table of showbread. She imagined him laying out the fresh loaves with deliberate care, each meticulously baked by their community's women. Every piece he arranged wasn't just bread but a symbol of sustenance and of Yahweh's providence, a silent hope for the continued blessings on their land.

She envisioned him at the altar of incense, lighting the blend of hallowed spices. She imagined the fragrant smoke spiraling upward, carrying the collective prayers of their people to the heavens. That sweet scent would permeate the sanctuary, bridging the holy with the everyday.

Throughout her day, Hannah pondered on Elkanah's responsibilities beyond the rituals. She considered his role in instructing their community, interpreting Yahweh's laws, and ensuring peace and order among their people. He settled disputes, offered wisdom, and was the spiritual beacon for those searching for guidance.

Hours from now, when dusk draped the sky, she knew Elkanah would perform the evening rituals akin to those at dawn. Once again, the menorah would be nurtured, old bread replaced with fresh offerings, and a new round of incense ignited. His day would culminate at the laver, where he started the day, and where he would wash away his service's tangible and intangible exertions.

Throughout these musings, Hannah felt a deep sense of pride. Elkanah was not just fulfilling a duty. He was embracing a divine privilege. As a servant of Yahweh, a steward of His teachings, and a guiding light, his demanding role had a profound purpose. It was a testament to the sacred bond between Yahweh and the Levites. More than that, between Yahweh and His people.

Hannah moved back into the tent, her hands working almost automatically to prepare herself for the choir. The soft rustling of the tent flaps and the muffled voices outside created a distant hum, a backdrop to her inner thoughts.

Suddenly, a louder commotion broke through. She paused, listening, and discerned the familiar voices of Eli's sons, Hophni and Phinehas. Their tones were demanding, edged with entitlement.

She pushed the tent flap aside, peering out. Some watchers were engaged in a heated argument with the two men. The contention was apparent. The sons of Eli, in their arrogant defiance of tradition and propriety, insisted on roasted meat. They wanted it before the rightful time, before the fat had been offered to the Lord in flame, and before the boiling.

She could see the priest's servant, caught between duty and the aggressive demands of these wayward sons. His face held both fear and frustration. To Hannah, the blatant disrespect of these two was not merely about meat but about the sanctity of their rituals.

Hannah felt both anger and sadness. Eli's sons, born to lead and guide, were squandering their inheritance, eroding the people's faith. Her fingers tightened around the tent's fabric. Here she was, yearning for a child to dedicate to the

Lord, while those born into the privilege treated it with contempt.

With a sigh, she pulled back, resuming her preparations. She held a quiet prayer in her heart, not just for herself but for the community, that they might find the strength and wisdom to navigate these testing times.

Simeon stepped into the tent, his brows knitted in confusion. He had caught the tail end of the altercation.

"I do not understand," he began, looking to Hannah for clarity. "Why does it matter so much how the meat is prepared? Boiled or roasted, is it not all for Yahweh anyway?"

Hannah paused before answering, measuring her words carefully. "It is not just about the method, Simeon. It is about obedience, reverence, and the profound connection between us and Yahweh."

Simeon looked puzzled. "But if the goal is to honor Him, then the specifics should not matter, right?"

Hannah sighed. "Think of it this way. If you were to make a promise to a friend, would the details of that promise matter?"

"Well, yes," Simeon admitted.

"Exactly," Hannah continued. "Yahweh has provided us with guidelines, not to restrict us but to show us the best way to honor and connect with Him. These rituals and traditions are not mere formalities. They carry the wisdom and legacy of our ancestors. They remind us of our covenant."

Simeon pondered her words, glancing back outside where the dispute occurred. "It is more than just a meal, then."

"It always is, Simeon. It always is."

The tent's fragile peace was interrupted as the flap rustled violently, and Ayala, distraught and with tears staining her face, burst in. The atmosphere immediately shifted.

Hannah was quick to approach, her maternal instincts kicking in. "Ayala, what is wrong? Are you not feeling well?"

Between sobs, Ayala choked out her words. "It is not me, Hannah. It is my cousin. She was assisting her abba at the tabernacle, and Eli's sons… They…they assaulted her."

Simeon's face flushed with anger. "This cannot go on! Someone has to put a stop to their wickedness!"

Every bit of Hannah's core was as tight as the skin of a drum before the strike. "Simeon," she said firmly, "we cannot combat such darkness with force alone. But there is another way."

Ayala looked up, her tear-filled eyes searching Hannah's for answers.

Hannah continued, "This heat, this anger we feel, we can channel it into something more potent than any show of strength." She closed her eyes and took a deep breath, the swelling heat in her heart transforming into a purposeful flame. "Join me, both of you. Let us bring our pain, anger, and hope together in prayer. Only through Yahweh can we find the strength to confront such evil and guide our people back to righteousness."

They joined hands, forming a circle of solidarity. Hannah began, her voice clear and unwavering.

"Oh Yahweh, our shelter and our strength, in times of chaos and despair, we turn to You. Guard the innocent, protect those who suffer at the hands of wickedness, and guide those who have gone astray back to Your righteous path.

"For in Your wisdom, we find clarity. In Your love, we find solace. And in Your justice, we find hope. May the deeds of the wicked be exposed, and may our hearts remain steadfast in faith, seeking only Your guidance."

Ayala and Simeon echoed her sentiments with a soft "Amen," their spirits perhaps lifted, if only slightly, by the shared act of faith and unity. Hannah hoped they took comfort in the power of prayer, trusting that their heartfelt pleas would not go unheard. *Yahweh, make a way....*

CHAPTER FOURTEEN

Hannah stood in the heart of the courtyard of the tent of meeting. Her emotions waged within her like the clash of swords and shields in the heat of battle. Sacred anticipation filled the air. Her skin prickled.

Being one of the singers today was a great honor and a responsibility. Dressed in white linen, Hannah stood with the others. As her eyes fixed on the sacred scrolls, her fingertips traced the embroidery of her sash. The calming motion steadied her nerves. Elkanah had used his influence to ensure an invitation was extended to her. The thought of it caused a smile to curl on her lips. He had always cared for her well. Hannah's mind flitted back to when they first met—he a musician and she a singer in this very place, during the same yearly festival.

At Eli's cue, the music commenced. The dulcet tones of the harps wafted through the courtyard of the tabernacle, enveloping Hannah's spirit. Flutes joined the strings, their notes weaving into the melody, adding layers to the sacred atmosphere. The rhythm of the tympanum echoed in sync with Hannah's heartbeat, a pulsating reminder of her inner turmoil.

Even though Hannah could not see him from where she stood, she pictured Elkanah with the silver trumpet lifted to his lips, prepared for the moment he would join in. Her heart pounded with trepidation and exhilaration, like the march-ing of the Israelite warriors, strong and resolute yet and in awe of the divine. Her emotions—fear, hope, and joy—were a symphony directed by the unseen hand of faith.

Soon, the silver trumpets would burst forth, their clear, resonant tones cutting through the rich symphony of sound. Elkanah's note would be among them, a bright beam of melody that would pierce her very being. And at that moment, Hannah's heart would leap within her like the shout of victory from the walls of a conquered city, resonant and triumphant.

Yet she could not think of that now. Hannah's eyes fixed on the choir director. This was the time for Hannah to lend *her* voice to the sacred song. Drawing a deep breath, she watched the director. When she gave the cue, Hannah opened her mouth and let the notes flow. Her voice rose strong and clear, joining the others, lifting together like a wave.

> Let the sound of praise rise like incense, a sweet
> offering to You,
> For those who trust in the Lord shall never be put to
> shame.
> In the morning, may they awake with songs of
> thanksgiving;
> At night, let them rest in the assurance of Your
> unending love.
> Grant them the courage to face the trials of the day,
> With faith unshaken, hope unbroken, love unending.
> Lead them beside still waters, refresh their weary souls,

Nourish them with the bread of life; quench their
thirst with living streams.

As her voice rose and fell in the sacred rhythm, Hannah
closed her eyes and imagined their praise rising over the tent
and carrying on the wind before drifting down like rain into
the Holy of Holies, where Yahweh resided. Hannah's heart and
soul soared as if lifted on the wings of seraphs. Her spirit lifted
higher with each note. This was more than singing. This was a
prayer, an offering, a testament to their unwavering faith.

The song echoed around the tabernacle, carried by the
afternoon breeze. Daring to open her eyes, Hannah turned to
scan the crowd. Her gaze swept over the family units gathered
in clusters. She searched for Peninnah, the children, and their
servants, but she did not see them.

Even as the priests stepped forward to offer the ritual sacrifice, the words she had sung continued to weave through
Hannah's mind. *"Grant them the courage to face the trials of the
day...."* Something stirred inside as if awakening after a long
slumber.

Grant me, yes, grant me the courage to face the trials of the day.

Hannah clasped her hands together and then pressed them
to her lips. Her heart fluttered like the wings of the dove that
had risen from Noah's hands, lifting in search of life after
destruction. Then, as if taken back to the moment when Elkanah
confessed to her that he was betrothed to Peninnah and would
be marrying again, she considered the past few years.

EXTRAORDINARY WOMEN of the BIBLE

Remembering the news that Peninnah carried a child soon after becoming Elkanah's second wife, Hannah felt tears begin to form. They flowed softly at first, then grew in intensity. Yet even with the tears falling, Hannah continued to sing. Continued to praise.

As Peninnah's stomach had grown with the child, so had her often hurtful words, as well as those of some members of their community. And when four sons followed the first daughter, it was as if the fountains of the deep broke. The cracks spread, growing broader and deeper, bringing destruction and chaos where once there was solid ground.

Soon Hannah could no longer recognize her life, marriage, or self. How long had she been adrift, battered by sorrow and doubt? So long that she had forgotten what standing on a firm foundation felt like. She knew that Elkanah loved her. Favored her even, despite her inability to give him what he most desired. Yet that love had never been enough. Yahweh's love had never been enough. She saw that now.

Noah's hope had no doubt been fragile when he, adrift in an infinite sea, released a dove into the sky. Yet perhaps the smallest part of him trusted that it would find land. It was a leap of faith amid uncertainty, a belief in something greater beyond the visible horizon.

Hope now beckoned Hannah to release her fears and doubts. Hope urged her to embrace the possibility that even in her darkest moments, there was a path forward, a new beginning waiting to be uncovered. It was the conviction that, though the waters might be deep and the journey long, if she dared to send forth her dove, trusting in what she could not yet see, she might find that solid ground was nearer than she thought.

As she sang, Hannah lifted her fists. Slowly she unfurled her fingers as she released the pain. She had been wearing it as a shroud too long. In that moment the music rose, and in Hannah's soul a glimmer of light began to shine in the darkness. From the depths of her soul, a new melody of praise emerged. It was fragile and faint yet full of purity and grace that transcended her pain. Her mind dared to hope. Her heart began to believe that maybe, just maybe, not all was lost.

She lifted her eyes to the heavens. Could Yahweh answer her prayer still, if she would only ask Him? Could He reach down into the brokenness and mend what was shattered? Could He bring life to the wasteland, joy to the mourning, peace to the storm?

Hannah's praise continued to rise, a sweet offering to the One who, she now knew, had never forsaken her. And as she sang, a warmth enveloped her, a presence that whispered promises of love, redemption, and restoration. In that sacred moment, Yahweh was with her. He heard her cry. He would answer in His time and His way.

With hope in her heart, Hannah stepped forward into the unknown, putting her trust in Yahweh, who alone knew what the future held. He could make all things new.

Hannah now saw the tabernacle as if for the first time. The curtains were vibrant, the blue symbolizing heaven and Yahweh's presence, while the scarlet symbolized sacrifice. The pure white curtains swayed in the wind, adding to the heavenly feel of the place.

Around her, the songs from the choir and the melodic chants of the Levites harmonized into one. Then, like a lightning bolt of sound, the resonant blasts of the priests' trumpets punctuated the air, marking the next phase of the sacred ceremony.

Upon direction, the choir moved forward as one, pausing before the gathering of Levites and priests who were lined up in their white linen robes. Then, like the stilling of a thunderstorm, the voices and the music faded into silence. With bated breath, the singers and Levites, the people and priests, waited for the invocation.

With a strong voice, the high priest's powerful words rose above the crowd. A sea of faces focused on him as he proclaimed their holy position as those chosen to be part of a lineage of faith that stretched from Abraham to Jacob and beyond.

After offering a remembrance of their journey through history as Yahweh's chosen people, Eli's words transformed into a song.

From the whispering winds to the sands beneath;
From the soaring skies to the waters that seethe;
His hand has been with us, His covenant true.
We are the bearers of faith; we are the chosen few.

With those words, "the chosen few," the choir joined in, followed by the voices of the people. Their unified song, a blend of praise and plea, invoked Yahweh's strength, guidance, and mercy. The poignant melodies married with rising incense, lifting together to the heavenly realms.

As the verses ebbed and flowed, Hannah felt her spirit lift, reconnecting her with her roots and Yahweh's bond.

Through the blood of the lamb on doorways marked,
Moses declared, "To God we impart
Every firstborn son, a sacred gift."
Passover's promise, through times, does sift.

"Consecrate each firstborn, to Me they belong;
From every womb among the tribes so strong.
Both man and beast, under the sacred sign,
In each consecration, the divine and man align."

As Hannah sang, the melodies intertwined with her new revelation, causing the thoughts and prayers of the past twenty years to overturn within her soul. Her previous prayers had not been offerings of submission to the Divine Will but merely echoes of her own wants.

Hannah pulled in a deep breath and released it with a prayer. *Lord, here I am. Here are all my hopes too.* The words lifted from her heart, releasing on the breath of a song.

Words came unbidden to her consciousness, a whisper in the wind. The words spoken so long ago to Moses.

"You shall give Me the firstborn among your sons."

CHAPTER FIFTEEN

A s the day bowed to the evening's embrace, the once-busy surroundings of the sacred place began to quiet, with most of Yahweh's devoted followers retiring to their tents, leaving behind the echo of their fervent prayers and worship. The air was still thick with the residue of incense, which combined with the scent of burnt offerings and the rich aroma of herbs and spices. It was a time of sacrifice and thanksgiving.

In their dwelling, Hannah took her place beside Elkanah. His reassuring smile was a soothing balm. Together, they sat on low cushions, assembled around a large wooden table laden with dishes showcasing the land's bounty.

Roasted lamb, spiced barley bread, olives drenched in aromatic oils, plump figs, succulent dates, and a bowl of lentil stew spiced with cumin adorned the table.

Elkanah began their feast with a prayer of gratitude. He tore a piece of bread and passed it around, and when Hannah received her piece, the warmth of the bread felt like the embrace of an old friend. As she dipped it into the lentil stew, its earthy taste reminded her of simpler times.

Bitter herbs lay on each plate, symbolizing the bitterness of slavery their ancestors endured in Egypt, contrasting sharply with the sweet *charoset*, reminding them of the mortar used in forced labor. At other tables there were heartfelt psalms and prayers of gratitude echoing into the night.

After clearing his throat, Elkanah began the traditional blessings. "Blessed are You, Yahweh our God, King of the Universe, who has sanctified us with His commandments and commanded us concerning the Passover sacrifice," he recited with reverence. The gravity of his words, a legacy of their forefathers, enveloped them all.

Elkanah's voice once again rose in song, this time a melody composed specially for Passover. The lyrics, steeped in history and faith, swirled around them.

"Yahweh, our guide, strength, and song, led us from bondage, where we were wronged. With a mighty hand and an outstretched arm, He guided our path and protected us from harm."

As the song unfurled, Hannah was enveloped in contemplation. In the depth of her being, a prayer formed—a completion of her surrender to Yahweh.

When the song concluded, a silence prevailed. Yet the echo of faith remained. Hannah and Elkanah exchanged a look, an unspoken bond of shared faith, love, and hope in Yahweh's grand design.

Elkanah prepared to distribute portions of the sacrificial meal. She knew he would save the meat for last. The food was not mere sustenance but a tangible testament to Elkanah's steadfast love, promising his family would never suffer hunger or deprivation.

When Elkanah approached her, his pace slowed, and warmth emanated from his gaze. He offered her a double portion. It was more than a gesture of tradition. It was a silent proclamation of his enduring love. While others would see this as the mark of favor that it was, to Hannah, it deepened her resolve. So intense were her emotions that tears once again began to form.

Her husband cleared his throat again. "Hannah." His voice was gentle, soothing like a cool breeze on a scorching day.

He sat on the cushion next to her. His large hand wrapped around her small one. "Why do you cry? You must eat." He released her hand and touched her cheek. "Why does sorrow overcome you? Am I not more valuable to you than ten sons?"

She could not answer. Only yesterday, she might have longed to hear him say, *You, Hannah, are better to me than ten sons.* But today she did not need to hear those words. The tenderness in her husband's gaze bore the weight of his unwavering devotion.

"Thank you, Husband," Hannah managed. "I am caught in the grip of feelings from the day." She ate a few bites of the meat.

Elkanah commenced dispensing the portions. Hannah glanced around at Peninnah and her children, who were eagerly awaiting their feast.

She could not stay. She needed solitude, a moment alone to pour out her soul, to whisper her deepest longings and fears into the ears of the Creator. It could wait no longer.

"I need fresh air," she said, rising.

Elkanah stared at her quizzically but merely nodded.

Once outside, she felt the weight of conviction. There was only one place to go. The tabernacle.

There, the veil between the divine and the mortal was thin, where the whispers of her heart would rise like sweet fragrance to the heavens.

Her short journey to the tabernacle was not merely a physical one but also a spiritual pilgrimage. She would seek solace and understanding in the presence of the Divine. She would connect, lay bare her soul, and find refuge in the shadow of the Most High. She would experience the peace that spoke louder than the clamor of the world outside.

The silence that surrounded the tabernacle as she approached was not emptiness but a comforting presence, a sacred space where Hannah could unfold her heart's deepest layers, seeking the compassion and love of Yahweh.

In Hannah's soul was a new, selfless melody.

A child for Your purpose, not just for mine.
I've yearned for solace, for shame to flee,
But missed Your wisdom, Your holy decree.

The words ran through her mind. Words she hoped to share with Elkanah later. Maybe he could even help her compose a song.

To fulfill Your command, to align with the Divine,
To consecrate the firstborn, in Your holy design;
A child not just for love or to erase my shame,
But a life dedicated to glorifying Your name.

At the tabernacle's entrance, anticipation surged within her. In a moment of pure reverence, her heart and soul converged in worship, her prayers interlacing with those of generations past and future. A growing hope whispered that her pleas would find favor and her sorrow be turned into joy.

Hannah's feet felt heavy, the ground rough beneath her sandals. The people around her seemed distant and unreal, their faces blurred by her tears, though she could hear their murmured prayers. A desperate need burned within her, a yearning that could not be silenced. How many times had she prayed for a child? Too many to count. Yet today a new urgency stirred.

"You shall give Me the firstborn among your sons."

The words Yahweh had spoken to her repeated in her mind, as they had since her earlier experience in the choir.

But she had no child. She must pray, seeking clarity from Yahweh Himself.

Eli, the high priest of the Lord, sat by the doorpost. His weathered gaze met Hannah's. Did he see the silent anguish in her soul?

Her heart pounded as she approached the old priest, the words of her prayer forming and reforming in her mind. Her hands trembled and her lips quivered as she steeled herself to pray, to trust.

Her lips were dry, her throat tight. She found a quiet space near the entrance, her body trembling as she knelt, her hands clasped tightly together. Head bowed, eyes closed, she knew that before she could pray with all her heart, she must allow the pain to wash over her, a tide of sorrow that even now threatened to overwhelm her, and out into Yahweh's waiting hands.

"Why, O Lord?" she whispered, her voice breaking, her words barely audible. "Why have You made me thus? Why have You given me breasts if not to nurse a child? Why have You planted this desire within me, leaving it unfulfilled?"

She knew that others looked at her with pity and saw her as incomplete, a woman marred by her barrenness. But they could not see the emptiness that gnawed at her heart, the void that no amount of love or support ever filled.

This time, her prayer was not just a cry from her heart but a pledge to align her desire with the Divine's. Sniffling the cries back inside, Hannah continued to pray. Her lips moved, but no sound emerged.

She laid her soul bare before Yahweh.

The dark days of the past few years flashed through Hannah's mind. She thought of the nights she slept alone without the warmth of her husband at her side. She considered the moments she cried alone by the brook in the woods. She thought of the days she hid away in her bed even during the daylight hours, not able to face the happy smiles of immas and children.

And then, as if gazing upon herself with the view of a hawk from above, Hannah saw a different image. A vessel that Yahweh was emptying for the purpose of filling it with Himself—what her heart truly desired.

Within this hallowed place, where every inch of ground resonated with the breath of Yahweh, Hannah found herself enveloped in a tempest of sorrow mixed with awe. No longer able to hold back her tears, she felt the deep anguish of her soul split open, and she cried bitterly as she prayed.

Her agony poured from her, a cascade of sobs and tears, a fervent, heartfelt plea. "O Lord of Heaven's Armies, if You will look upon my sorrow and answer my prayer, bestowing a son upon me, I vow to dedicate him back to You. For his entire lifetime, he will be a symbol of Your grace, his hair a testament to his divine dedication, never to be cut."

Tears welled in Hannah's eyes as she spoke, her voice barely above a whisper. "I have wanted this child for *me*, to make me feel fulfilled, to bring me joy. But today, I ask not for myself but for Your desire. If You grant me a child, I shall dedicate him to You all the days of his life."

Moments later, she knew she had experienced a catharsis. She had laid bare her soul to Yahweh. She had made Him a promise she would keep, if her prayer was granted. And now she felt drained but also light, as if something so intangible as sorrow and bitterness had physical weight that she no longer carried.

She filled her lungs with the sweet air of peace.

She rose. She had the sensation of being watched intently.

Eli. A flurry of thoughts swirled in her mind. *Does he pity me? Does he see me as just another desperate soul seeking divine favors?*

Eli's words were not of comfort but of sharp rebuke. "Must you come here drunk?" he demanded. "Put away your wine!"

His words were like cold water thrown on her fervent prayers, making her flinch. Knowing what she knew of Eli and his sons, she should not have expected more from him. But this?

"I am not a wicked woman. I have not been drinking wine or anything stronger," she said. "I have been praying out of great anguish and sorrow." Her words were simple and honest.

Eli's features softened, replacing the initial harshness. "In that case," he said, "go in peace. May the God of Israel grant the request you have asked of Him." His words were like a soothing balm on her wounded soul. There was good in this man.

"I thank you." She felt a rush of relief and gratitude, a flame of new hope in her heart. Gently, Hannah wiped away the residue of her tears. Her spirit felt liberated, her soul caressed by the warmth of hope. She knew she could go back and eat now. It no longer mattered what Peninnah or anyone else said or did or thought about her. The priest had given her a blessing. And she knew that Yahweh heard her prayer.

CHAPTER SIXTEEN

After the journey home, Hannah returned to the familiar rhythm of her daily life, now wrapped in a newfound hope and an unanticipated sense of peace. But while her heart felt lighter, the dynamics at home remained unchanged.

Hannah stood in the kitchen, where the warm glow of a flickering oil lamp cast long shadows on the clay walls. The comforting aroma of freshly baked bread pervaded the air while a pot of rich stew bubbled softly over the fire.

Hannah, her fingers dusted with flour, worked more dough diligently, letting its elasticity provide a momentary distraction. For a brief moment, she allowed herself to get lost in the beauty of the outside world. She sighed. "Peninnah, the sun sets in hues of gold today, does it not?"

Without missing a beat, Peninnah responded, the simmering stew mirroring her simmering resentment. "Oh, Hannah, every day must surely seem beautiful to you. Living as the favored one, the recipient of endless blessings and admiration. Tell me, how does it feel to be so revered?"

Hannah paused, taking a breath and choosing her words carefully. It was long past time that she have this conversation with her husband's second wife. "Peninnah, there is no need for such bitterness. We both share in the blessings of this home."

Hannah's fingers continued to shape the dough. "You know not the weight of this burden. To feel the emptiness and yearning. A husband's love, though wondrous, cannot fill an empty womb. It cannot silence the whispers of shame and the judgments of others."

Peninnah's usual defiant posture softened, her hand stilled over the simmering pot. A ripple of surprise flashed across her face, quickly replaced by an expression of unusual uncertainty. The stirring stick in her hand slowed its circular motion.

"Hannah," Peninnah began, her voice losing some of its previous sharpness, "I did not mean…"

She trailed off, her eyes narrowing as she apparently searched for the right words. The silence stretched between them, the only sound being the low simmer of the stew and the distant hum of the evening crickets outside.

"To upset you," she finally managed to say, her gaze darting away from Hannah. She turned her attention back to the stew. "I know I can be…difficult at times," she admitted, a hint of remorse threading through her words.

In the dimly lit tent, the crackling of the hearth seemed louder than usual, punctuating the stillness that hung in the air. Hannah could feel the weight of Peninnah's presence, the intensity of her gaze fixed on the glowing embers.

Peninnah's facade crumbled for a fleeting moment, revealing a rarely displayed depth. The warm firelight illuminated her profile, casting a mosaic of light and shadow upon her features. "Perhaps…perhaps I should try to be more understanding," she murmured, her voice laced with a vulnerability she seldom showed. "After all, we are both bound by Elkanah's love."

Hannah remembered her fervent prayer, the priest's words, the promise of hope. The rich, yeasty scent of the rising dough mingled with the intensity of her feelings.

She paused, her fingers pressing, shaping the soft mass meticulously. "Peninnah, my solace is not found merely in the love of a husband. I have anchored my hope in something far greater." She breathed deeply, her voice steadying, a hint of tears shimmering but not falling. "I trust in Yahweh. Even amid this tribulation, I believe He has a plan for me. My faith is where I find refuge."

Peninnah's gaze lingered on Hannah, a flash of unspoken understanding passing between them. "Perhaps," she said slowly, "we each have our journey with the Almighty, a path that we must tread, regardless of the shadows and the light that fall upon us."

CHAPTER SEVENTEEN

Life continued in a familiar routine for Hannah, the sun rising and setting in its steady rhythm, each day filled with her usual tasks and duties. She threw herself into helping Ayala and tending to her household, but a subtle shift in her spirit started drawing her attention inward.

One day, as she helped prepare the meal, a sudden rush of sickness left her grasping the edge of the table. She wondered briefly if she had overexerted herself, stretching her capacities thin. But a whisper of hope, delicate and fragile, suggested a different possibility.

As the days went on, every flutter in her stomach made her wonder. She scrutinized every sensation while hope and worry intermingled in her thoughts. She noticed more and more— the sickness in the morning, the exhaustion, each symptom like a beacon, flashing the possibilities in front of her, whispering the unspoken dreams in her ears. The visible signs were there, but the shadow of past disappointments made her hesitant.

But finally the whispers grew louder, the signs more pronounced, and Hannah found she could no longer ignore the hope growing within her.

This morning, Hannah was awake before anyone else in the household stirred. One handed rested on the rough-hewn table while the fingers of the other tentatively explored her abdomen.

When she heard the gentle shuffle of Elkanah's feet and the sighing of the floorboards, she turned to him. The remnants of sleep still lingered on his face, softening his features, his dark curls a little disheveled.

"Hannah?" His voice was a whisper, a quiet concern in his tone. His eyes met hers, revealing the interweaving threads of hope and worry, mirroring her turbulent emotions.

Her heart ached to ease his long-held desire. But the fear crept in, whispering doubts, making her cautious to utter the words. What if she was wrong? What if the whispered promise turned out to be just a fleeting illusion? What if the new life she felt blossoming within her was taken away?

She closed her eyes for a moment, seeking solace, seeking strength. She thought of Eli's words, his promise of divine blessing, his assurance of her prayers being heard.

When she opened her eyes, she met Elkanah's hopeful gaze, the unspoken questions and concealed excitement shimmering. Had he an inkling of what she was about to reveal?

With a breath to steady her voice and a silent prayer for strength, she spoke. "Elkanah, I think… I believe…we may be blessed soon."

She could see the spark of hope intensify in his eyes, could feel the unspoken joy taking tentative steps in his soul, but she could also see the shadow of worry, the silent fear of disappointment that had dogged them their entire married life.

Elkanah continued to hold her gaze. "What are you saying?"

"I...I think I might be with child," she confessed.

The room fell silent, save for the crackling fire and the soft rustle of leaves outside. The corners of his mouth lifted in a tentative smile. "And why do you think this?" Elkanah's voice, usually so confident, wavered slightly.

"I feel...different. My body tells me." Her voice was barely above a whisper.

A silent understanding passed between them.

"The Lord has heard our prayers," he said softly, his voice trembling with barely suppressed emotion. He reached out to touch her cheek, his hand warm and comforting.

Inside, a whirlwind of feelings battled. Hannah felt an overwhelming sense of relief and a creeping sense of anxiety. She tasted the sweet tang of hope and the bitter sting of fear. But most of all, she felt a strong sense of faith, a firm belief that they were not alone in this journey.

"Yes," she agreed, her hand finding his, their fingers interlacing. "He has, but..."

Hannah pulled away gently and looked up at him. "There is more, Elkanah. I made a vow to the Lord. If He granted me a son, I would dedicate him to the Lord's service all the days of his life."

Elkanah's face fell, confusion and concern replacing his previous joy. The atmosphere around them was tense. "Hannah, what have you done?" His voice was strained.

Hannah met his gaze, her eyes shimmering with resolve and sorrow. "I prayed to the Lord," she began, the words weaving through the charged air between them, "and I made a vow."

Elkanah ran a hand down his beard and began to pace. His hands clenched unconsciously at his sides.

"What did you say, Hannah? What was your vow?" He stopped pacing to stare at her.

Taking a deep breath, Hannah felt her chest tighten. "I promised that if I was given a son, I would dedicate him for his lifetime to Yahweh."

Elkanah shook his head. "Why would you pledge our son in a Nazirite vow, Hannah?" She could tell he tried to mask the storm within him.

Hannah, her eyes wet with unshed tears, said, "Elkanah, my heart and my womb have been barren. I have been ridiculed, my spirit crushed under the weight of my childlessness." She paused, taking another deep breath as if drawing strength from the air around her. "I yearn to bear a child, to feel life grow within me, to bring forth a being from our union.

"I made a Nazarite vow because it symbolizes total dedication to the Lord. A representation of separation and holiness unto Him. Our son will be a blessed servant of the Lord, dedicated from the womb to the day of his death." She bit her lower lip. "I am not sure why, but the words just came out, 'Give me a son, I will give him back to You.'"

"Give him back? What do you mean, 'give him back'?" Elkanah questioned, his brows knitted together, his voice full of confusion and hurt. The air was heavy with unsaid words and unseen thoughts, a whirlwind of emotions engulfing them.

Hannah met his eyes, steadying herself. "I will take him to the tabernacle, to Shiloh, and leave him there to serve the Lord under Eli." Hannah was surprised by the conviction in her words. Divine commitment and maternal love swirled within her.

"You would leave our son in the tabernacle?" Elkanah's voice betrayed a hint of disbelief amid the pain. "To be raised by Eli, whose own sons are corrupt, who have turned away from God?"

"Yes," Hannah replied, her voice firm yet tinged with sorrow. "This is the vow I made. Our son will be dedicated to the Lord throughout his life."

Hannah could see Elkanah wrestling with a tide of emotions. "Did you not think about the ramifications? You speak of dedicating our child to the Lord, but do you truly understand what that entails?"

"I understand the magnitude, Elkanah," she answered, her voice steadied by the resolve within her. "It is a sacrifice I am willing to make to fulfill the vow I made."

"And what if you are not with child?" Elkanah's voice softened, a hint of sadness mingling with the lingering frustration. "What if there is no child to dedicate? What if the child is a girl? Then this conversation, this pain, will be for naught."

Grappling with the enormity of the situation, Hannah spoke with a resolute spirit, "If the Lord chooses not to bestow upon us a child, then I will endure that pain. But if He blesses us, I am bound by my vow."

"But to relinquish our child, Hannah." The struggle was evident in Elkanah's voice, a cracking resonance accompanied by eyes glazed with moisture. "To forgo witnessing his growth, to be absent from his journey. Does the Lord truly require such a heart-wrenching sacrifice from us?"

The internal battle raging within Elkanah was painfully evident in his face, causing her heart to ache. Elkanah, always so knowledgeable in the laws of Moses, seemed entangled in his thoughts, struggling between his duties as a husband, his love for her, and his unwavering faith in Yahweh.

"You know the laws of vows far better than I do." Her words were soft but laced with sorrow and firm resolve. "If you deem it right to nullify my vow, it will be as you say, according to the laws given by Moses. If you hear of my vow and remain silent, the vow is valid. But if you annul it after hearing it, God will release me from the vow."

Elkanah pulled back his shoulders and adopted the demeanor of an instructor, his gaze intense as he peered deep into Hannah's eyes, studying her as if she were a scroll of the law, each word, each emotion, a verse to be deciphered. The storm within him was evident, a torrent of emotions battling as he deliberated over the profound implications of the law Hannah had invoked. "The choice is mine, then."

Barely above a whisper and laden with tears yet to fall, Hannah replied, "Yes, my love. Your silence is the seal to my vow and your disapproval, my liberation."

Elkanah was visibly torn, wrestling internally with the unspoken words and the possible outcomes of his decision. His deep knowledge of the law only heightened the intensity of their silent exchange, with each word unspoken carrying the weight of obligation and love, faithfulness, and surrender.

A part of Hannah yearned for him to voice his disagreement, to release her from the vow she had made, but another part knew the consequences of toying with vows made to Yahweh. This was no game, no battling with wooden swords. The stakes were real.

"You would be releasing me from my promise." Hannah's voice shook, and she clenched her hands at her side. "The burden would indeed be upon you. The guilt of annulling a vow to the Lord will not be light."

The air between them was charged with unsaid words, unshed tears, and unmade decisions. Only the strength of her conviction kept her own guilt at bay. She had put her beloved husband in the position of making an impossible decision.

"This is the promise I made," Hannah continued. "I pray you understand. It is not about pain or sacrifice. It is about dedicating our child to the service of the Lord. It is my faith, *our* faith in the Lord's plans."

Elkanah paused and turned to her. "You make this vow as though my guidance is not enough for our child." His voice was strained. "Do you not trust me to raise our son in the Lord's ways?"

Hannah saw the tumult in his eyes, the battle between his sacred obligations as a watcher and her sacred promise. "It is not about trust in you," she whispered. "This is a vow to the Lord, a dedication of our hoped-for son to Him. It is not a reflection on you or your guidance."

"I will say it again. To dedicate him to the tabernacle is to leave him under Eli's care," Elkanah countered sharply, his brow furrowed in frustration. "A man who has failed his own sons. Is that the guidance you wish for our child?"

Hannah met his gaze, her eyes brimming with unshed tears. "This is not about Eli, Elkanah. This is about dedicating our son to the service of the Lord. It is a commitment I do not undertake lightly." Her chest tightened with every word, the sorrowful reality of her vow weighing heavily upon her heart.

"I feel dishonored, Hannah." Elkanah pulled away, his movements stiff. "As if you believe I am not capable of guiding our son in righteousness."

"It pains me to see you hurt, my love," Hannah replied, her voice breaking. "But a promise to the Lord surmounts our earthly desires and pains."

Elkanah turned, his face a canvas depicting utter torment, a tempest of emotions threatening to rip him apart. He was caught up in a silent, harrowing conflict between the sacredness of a vow not of his own making and the love for a child he might never fully claim. Hannah felt this conflict too. But her choice was already made. Her heart wept for him, for herself.

"I wish you had consulted me before making such a grave vow, Hannah." His voice was a whisper, but its pain and betrayal were louder than any shout could ever be. "A vow involving us both, especially one that concerns presenting our child to the tabernacle—for the Lord's service—should have been *our* decision, not yours alone."

Hannah felt a stab of pain at his words, but she knew he was right. "I did not fully understand the weight of my words until they were spoken." Tears rolled down her cheeks. "I was distraught, my heart heavy with sorrow, and I only wished for our pain to end. I promise it was not meant to undermine your role as an abba or as a husband."

Then again, we would not have this child if it were not for my vow.

Hannah could feel the weight of Elkanah's gaze, its usual warmth tinged with the lingering pain of their conversation. She could almost hear his thoughts racing, conflicting with his duty as a Levite and his love for her.

As he stepped closer, the air charged with silent emotions. His arms enveloped her, his embrace a sanctuary of love and safety, and she melted into him, seeking solace in his solid, familiar strength. The cool, tense air retreated before the comforting warmth that radiated from him.

"Hannah, my love," he said, the intimacy of the words wrapping around her like a comforting shawl, "seeing you in pain is unbearable, and the thought of you traversing this path terrifies me."

Closing her eyes, she submerged herself in the moment, relishing the comforting feel of his arms, the reassuring rhythm of his heartbeat echoing against her, providing a haven from the storm of emotions swirling around them. The world, with its chaos and pain, seemed to fall away, leaving them enclosed in a fragile bubble.

"I am so sorry," Hannah murmured into his chest, her body racked as sobs overtook her. "I would never want to hurt you. It was a plea, a desperate plea to the Lord."

They held each other, lost in their shared pain and love, seeking solace in each other's arms, their hearts connected yet facing a future unknown and unseen. Elkanah finally whispered, "Let us walk this path together, whatever may come."

"I love you more than words can express, and I cannot walk this path alone. I need you by my side," she responded, her voice muffled by his robe.

With a final squeeze, they slowly pulled away, their eyes locking, conveying love, pain, resolve—and a silent promise to face the future together, whatever it might hold.

CHAPTER EIGHTEEN

H annah, with her water jar cradled gently against her side, observed the changing shape of her shadow. Her growing silhouette was a beautiful announcement of the life growing within her, stirring a warm smile to her lips. On this day, the quaint village of Ramathaim-Zophim, with its surrounding lush hills and fertile fields, seemed to vibrate with a renewed energy and vivid color, or maybe, she mused, it was her heart unfolding, absorbing the beauty around her with newfound appreciation.

Each structure in the village, crafted from sun-kissed bricks and strong, enduring timber, spoke to her of promises of a protective and nurturing haven. Children's joyful laughter and playful shouts brought a melody of happiness and purity to this village. This place, where the simplicity of life flowered under the watchful gaze of spiritual guardians, seemed like an extension of heaven on earth.

Yet interlaced with her joy, a thread of sorrow wove through Hannah's spirit as she thought of her son. For she was sure this child *would* be a son. As she walked, the growing weight in her middle was a constant reminder of the blessings and future pains. Her son would not have the chance to feel and understand the embracing warmth of this village or the unity of his tribe, experience the familial bonds with his siblings, or his parents' tender, protective embrace.

A subtle movement stirred within, a gentle reminder of the precious life. Automatically, her hands caressed her belly, conveying unspoken love and sweet, comforting words to the unborn child. "May you feel the warmth of the sun, the joy in the air, and know the abundance of love that surrounds you, my dear one."

Her mind painted vivid images of the days to come, days when she would hold her boy—her own sweet boy—close to her chest, feeling his tiny heart beat in rhythm with hers, only to then endure the piercing pain of handing him over to another. The mere thought was like a physical ache, a tightening around her heart, a reflection of the impending separation. "Lord, grant me strength," she whispered, "to tread the path You have set before me, to endure the joys and the pains with grace, to shower this child with all the love and wisdom within me for as long as he is mine."

As she approached the well, Hannah hummed softly. Then her voice rose, singing the tunes that Elkanah had sung to his boys, a sweet lullaby of love and divine protection:

Rest now, my dear one, beneath the moon's soft glow.
Dream 'neath the twinkling stars that gently bestow.
Close those tender eyes, let the world fade away;
In dreams roam the lands where Yahweh's heroes stay.

Sleep, my precious, kissed by the night so sweet,
Hear the winds whisper tales where heaven and
    earth meet.

In dreams let your spirit with the breezy winds soar
To the gentle lullaby of the night, my dear, yearn for
     more.
May your dreams be sweet until the dawn does alight.

Rest, my love, in Abba's caring, loving embrace;
His arms are your refuge, filled with divine grace.
Though I cannot be there to hold you near and tight,
In your heart, may His love be your guiding light.

As the lullaby floated into the serene air, tears filled Hannah's eyes. Her tears were both gratitude and aching love—droplets that spoke the language of her soul.

Pausing before the well, Hannah set down her water jug and swiftly wiped the tears away, her heart entwined with sorrow and solace. Although she knew she would not be there to nurture her son each day, she found comfort and peace in a deep, unshakeable belief that Yahweh would be an abba to her child, wrapping him in an embrace of eternal love and divine protection.

This profound assurance acted as a soothing balm to her soul, whispering promises that divine love would surround her child. The whisper turned into a melodious prayer imbued with hope and faith under the watchful and loving eyes of the Creator.

Then another woman from the village approached the well, her eyes lighting up as she caught sight of Hannah's blooming form. "Blessings upon you, Hannah!" she exclaimed, her voice laced with joy and excitement. "Look at you! An imma-to-be! The heavens have indeed smiled upon you!"

Behind the first, a group of women approached with their water jugs and joined in the well-wishes. Some of these women had taunted her about her barrenness for so many years. Hannah now chose to forgive them and accept their congratulations and blessings. What good did holding on to bitterness and resentment do? Such negative emotions felt insignificant in the face of her impending joy.

Hannah received the blessings with a gracious smile, her heart swelling. Yet amid the shared jubilations, a shadow flitted across her mind. How would they react when she walked to the tabernacle with her child, only to return empty-handed? Would their congratulations turn to whispers of confusion, their smiles transform into frowns of pity? Would they think her addled? The thought sent a pang through her heart.

But she shook her head, choosing to lock those thoughts away, at least for now. Today, her child was hers, a sweet promise tucked safely within her womb. Today, she would bask in the sun's glow and in the shared joy of her community.

Hannah allowed herself to be submerged in the moment, drinking in the laughter, the stories, the gentle clinking of the water jars, and the soft murmurs of the breeze. Even before his birth, her son had already become a gift, a bridge bringing her closer to these women she had held at arm's length for so long. Tangled up in all these moments and emotions, Hannah found a fragile, beautiful peace, a treasure she held close to her heart, and she whispered silent thanks to the heavens above for this unexpected gift of companionship and unity.

As the women finished filling their jars, a figure rushed up to Hannah. Thirteen-year-old-Oren, Elkanah's second-born son, was a mirror image of his abba with the same thoughtful eyes and earnest expression. He reached to help her with the water jar, his hands gripping the vessel tightly.

"Thank you, Oren," Hannah said.

Hannah smiled. Oren was now taller than she, his shoulders broad and mature. His growth seemed swift, transitioning him from the boy who used to be engrossed in mock battles with Eitan to a young man easily carrying responsibilities. The games of youth were slipping away, and the training days loomed near, a rite of passage for every young man in the village.

Though each day was painted with serenity and the beauty of simple joys, a shadow lingered, a subtle whisper of the potential threat of the Philistines, like a distant storm cloud on a sunny day. It was a silent worry interwoven with every laugh, a subtle apprehension coloring the edges of every peaceful moment.

The evident transition in Oren, coupled with his impending induction into manhood and its responsibilities, only deepened the shadows lurking within Hannah's heart. Elkanah must be carrying worries for all his sons. Although his concerns often hid behind daily tasks and responsibilities, the constant threat of war—and the known corruption among the priests—was a heavy burden indeed. She felt it too.

As she looked into Oren's eyes, a mixture of pride and a poignant longing wrapped around her heart. Whispered tales of days gone by and days to come joined with silent prayers for peace and for protection for Oren and his brothers. And their half brother she carried in her womb.

Instead of moving toward the homeward path, Oren hesitated, and a flicker of something troubling crossed his face.

"What is it, my dear?" Hannah asked.

A usually articulate and open young man, Oren seemed to struggle to speak, his gaze shifting from her face to her belly to the ground.

Hannah decided to soothe his apparent concern. She thought she knew what this was about. "Oren," she said, her hand moving to her rounded stomach, "I am going to have a baby. Maybe you noticed?" she teased. "Nothing has changed. I still care for you, your brothers, and your sisters very much. I always will."

She felt another subtle fluttering in her abdomen, a gentle reminder of the life growing inside, and in that moment she realize she loved Oren, truly loved him as a son. *Lord, what a joy to love these children and to be loved by them.* Her heart seemed to double within her chest.

A quiet peace filled Oren's eyes. Then he quickly looked away and moved toward the pathway to their home. "I hit a snake with a stone yesterday." His shoulders straightened in pride. "I was in the hills taking water to our shepherds, and they showed me how to use a sling. They told me to come again tonight, and I can practice some more."

Hannah clapped her hands. "That is wonderful, Oren. Truly wonderful."

He smiled broadly, but as they reached the last rise leading to their home, Oren slowed his pace. He turned to look at her. His eyes, pools of inquisitive light, shimmered with questions.

"I see them whispering sometimes." He spoke softly. "Imma seems distant, like she is walking through another world. And Abba...he is different, changed."

The distance between the well and their home elongated with Oren's questions, each step heavy with unspoken thoughts. His eyes fixed on their home. "Everything is changing."

Hannah followed his gaze. The additional rooms Elkanah had built for Peninnah stood out, a physical reminder of the division within. A second small kitchen now belonged to Peninnah, severing the shared meals and the shared moments around the table. The changes, the added rooms, and the separate kitchens were not just physical alterations but symbols of a growing rift. The quiet the separate quarters brought was both a solace and a poignant reminder of the laughter and chaos she missed. Every quiet moment was full of both peace and longing—a craving for the cheerful din of children. For the children she had helped raise and the one she never would.

Oren sighed. "If there is to be a new baby," he said, "then why is our home under a shadow, and why is Abba so angry?"

Hannah paused and turned to him. Gently, she reached to brush his cheek with reassuring tenderness. "Oren, our hearts overflow with immense love and joy for this miracle of new life. This child is a promise, a gift from God. But with such blessings, there are also sacrifices we must make. Commitments we are bound to uphold." She hesitated, struggling to find the words to explain her desperate prayer, her solemn vow, and the impending requirement of dedicating her firstborn.

"Sometimes, the blessings we receive are intertwined with pain and sacrifice. Joy often comes hand in hand with sorrow. We must learn to live with this balance and remember that God's ways are not ours. As your abba has explained to us in the teaching of the Torah, Yahweh created light and separated it from darkness. Likewise, in our lives, joy and sorrow, light and shadow, are part of His divine plan. We need to embrace both, trusting in His wisdom. And we must also remember that He holds both in the palm of His hand."

Hannah could see the confusion, the search for under-standing, in Oren's eyes. She talked in riddles, she knew. But she and Elkanah had decided not to mention their son's dedication to tabernacle service to the rest of the children until the time came. Elkanah wanted his other children to love this new fam-ily member fully during the time they had him.

"Why can't blessings just be happy?" Oren asked, balling his free hand into a fist at his side. "Why can't our home be full of laughter again? Why can't we all be together as we used to be?"

A soft breeze blew strands of hair across Hannah's face. She had no words to offer. Her heart ached with a desire to preserve the innocence in his eyes, the purity in his soul. She would not be the only one hurting when she left her son in Shiloh. The realization hit her anew.

Hannah sighed, offering the only explanation she could give. "Sometimes, the most profound blessings require the most profound sacrifices. Your brother has a destiny, a purpose that we cannot comprehend. Yahweh has outlined a journey for him, and we must have faith. We have to trust in His plan, even if it brings tears to our eyes."

Oren seemed to wrestle with her words, turning them over in his mind. "But can Yahweh not alter His designs? Can He not see our desire to be a happy family?"

Then a new realization hit him. Oren gasped and took a step back. "Doda, you said my *brother*? How do you know? You cannot already know it is a boy."

"How do I know?" Hannah pressed her lips together and considered how to phrase her answer. Then she continued walking. Without hesitation, Oren moved in step with her.

"I just have a knowing that it is a boy. I prayed for a son, and here we are." Hannah patted her stomach, and then she reached over and gave Oren's hand a quick squeeze. "Elkanah's sons are the best young men I know." She smiled. "Why wouldn't I want one for my own?"

Oren's face brightened at her words. But just as quickly, his brows folded in contemplation. "I just want all of us to be happy," he whispered.

They were near their home now. The additional rooms cast long shadows upon the final steps before they moved toward separate doorways to enter their homes.

"I know, my love, and we will be. In our hearts, we will always be together. I will be your doda always." Emotion caught in her throat. "And I am thankful my child will have you as a big brother. Remember that."

CHAPTER NINETEEN

In the tranquil courtyard, tucked within the rolling hills, Hannah sat amid whispers of rustling leaves and blooming autumn flowers. The land around her seemed touched by the Divine. Despite the season, the sun still warmed the land, a reminder of the past summer days.

While taking in the beauty around her, Hannah busied herself with sorting and folding the freshly laundered baby blankets she had made over the previous months. As her fingers brushed over the fabric, she imprinted the blankets with her silent prayers.

Next to her, Ayala cradled her tiny daughter, a bundle of delicate wonder and divine design. With the fold of the last blanket, Hannah leaned closer, absorbing the infant's fragile beauty. She marveled at the delicate lashes and tiny, perfectly sculpted fingers and toes.

"Did I resemble her as an infant?" Ayala inquired, a hint of laughter in her voice as she gently traced her daughter's cheek.

Hannah smiled. "I did not spend much time with you when you were this small." Her voice was soft, tinged with regret.

A shadow of sadness passed over Ayala's features. "It must have been so hard for you—my birth—especially when you could have no children."

Hannah waved a hand, dismissing the thought. "Let us not talk about those days. So much good has come to me since then." Hannah reached out and lifted the tiny hand. The baby's fingers wrapped around hers. "Once you became a toddler, you made sure you could *not* be ignored. You were a force of nature!"

"Oh yes?" Ayala's eyes sparkled with curiosity and amusement. "But what types of trouble could I have gotten into?" She shrugged. "Surely not too much."

Hannah chuckled. "Well, what about when you decided to taste nearly every fruit recently picked from the orchard to see if they were sweet enough? Do you remember? You nearly sent your imma into a fit!"

"I remember. She found me with fruit juice all over my face and clothes." She shook her head, smiling at the memory.

"And then there was the time you climbed the tallest olive tree because you wanted to 'touch the sky' and would not come down until suppertime!" With laughter spilling out, Hannah shared more cherished memories with Ayala.

Ayala's laughter mingled with Hannah's, creating a song of joy within the serene courtyard. "I was quite the adventurous spirit, wasn't I? And just think, our children will journey through life as companions, exploring the world hand in hand."

Hannah sucked in a sharp breath. She pulled her finger from the baby's grasp and pretended to pick bits of chaff from her sleeve so she wouldn't have to meet Ayala's gaze. "It is a joy to share my time of pregnancy with you." Striving to hide her tears, she steered the conversation in another direction. Her hands rested protectively over her womb. "These days, my mind seems more a sanctuary for worries than for dreams," she confessed.

Ayala cleared her throat as if urging Hannah to look at her. Hannah did, and the young woman's gaze was full of empathy and understanding. "Your heart bears the weight of two decades of silent hopes and suppressed longing—all for this precious blessing." Ayala's voice grew soft yet firm, her words woven with strands of kindness and truth. "Remember what you once told me? About having Yahweh as one's firm foundation?" She gave a loving squeeze to Hannah's hand. Ayala's eyes reflected the golden autumn light. "With Him as our rock, we can weather any storm. Our worries and fears we can lay at His feet, trusting in His everlasting love and mercy to carry us through."

A moment of silence rested between them, the air around them carrying the scent of fallen leaves and the sound of Elkanah's lyre from across the courtyard. Somehow he had entered without their knowing.

Ayala's face then altered with a hint of a smile and a distant gaze as though lost in a cherished memory. "Abba used to sing a song over me," she said, her voice a gentle whisper in the cooling breeze. "'Yahweh is our refuge, our shelter in the storm. In His embrace, we find our warmth. In His love, we are reborn.'" She sang the melody, a delicate weave of nostalgia and love, her voice carrying the gentle strength and comforting warmth of the words.

Ayala's song faded into the whispering breeze. And at that moment, amid the shadows and light of the waning day, Hannah felt a renewed strength, a spark of divine hope kindling in her soul, reminding her of the promise of His eternal presence and unfailing love.

"Indeed, Ayala, the Lord is our anchor, even in the most turbulent seas of life."

The strumming of Elkanah's lyre harmonized with the echoes of the hills of Ephraim, the notes lingering like the delicate autumn leaves suspended in the breeze. Each strum was a whisper of love and impending loss.

Of course, Ayala did not understand. Only Hannah and Elkanah knew of the loss to come. But that day was not today. Today, the air was rich with the scent of autumn blooms and the taste of impending winter and they were all together. Today that was enough.

Beside Elkanah rested a flute, carved from a single piece of reed, and a small hand drum, its surface worn smooth from years of use, both silent. The usual musicians, Eitan and Oren, were with the other youth receiving battle training. When played together, these instruments created a symphony that transcended time and place.

The lyre alone carried the melody now. Though the song was one of praise, a heaviness laced its notes, adding a depth of emotion. Hannah closed her eyes, losing herself in the intricate beauty of the moment, feeling a profound connection to something beyond, something divine.

Elkanah began to sing.

To the glory of Your name, O Lord,
May those who seek refuge in You be glad.

May they always sing for joy and feel Your protection.
In the shadow of Your wings,
Let them find shelter and strength,
Guided by Your wisdom,
Walking in the path of righteousness and grace.
O Yahweh of mercy, hear the cries of the faithful.
Extend Your lovingkindness to those who call upon
　　Your name.
In times of trouble and despair, be their fortress and
　　shield.
May Your presence be a light unto their feet, a lamp to
　　guide their way.

Even with the music, the absence of Peninnah and her younger children left an almost palpable void in the air, the usual chorus of joy and youthful energy replaced with a silence that seemed to hold its breath. Their departure followed closely on the heels of Ayala giving birth, with Peninnah citing the need to tend to her ailing mother as the reason for her extended absence. However, Hannah couldn't help but suspect that her child's impending arrival drove Peninnah away.

The thought was like a thorn in Hannah's heart, adding a tinge of sorrow to her moments of anticipation and joy. Peninnah, who had long been the bearer of children for Elkanah, seemed to find it unbearable to witness Hannah receiving the blessing she had long monopolized. Hannah understood the unspoken pain hiding behind Peninnah's eyes, the unvoiced fear of losing her place in Elkanah's heart now that Hannah would give him the gift that Peninnah alone had been able to give him until now.

Hannah felt a sting at the thought that the youngest children wouldn't be present to welcome their new brother into the world, to share the first smiles, the first touches with him. Her heart ached for them and the bond that could have grown between them, which now seemed as fragile and transient as the autumn leaves wafting in the breeze around her.

Despite this, she quietly yearned for reconciliation, offering up a silent prayer that the arrival of her child could bridge the unseen chasms between them, healing old wounds and nurturing new bonds—bonds fortified with mutual respect and understanding. And as she silently wrestled with these thoughts, she whispered hopes for unity and love, offering them to the gentle winds to carry to the ears of the Divine.

When her abba's music ended, Ayala stood, settling the infant in her arms. "I should be on my way home."

Hannah leaned in to plant a tender kiss on the baby's forehead, promising stories and cuddles in the coming days. "Perhaps I will see you tomorrow. And may the Lord's favor shine upon you both until then." Ayala, cradling her treasure, disappeared down the dirt road to the village and her home.

The peaceful scene was soon interrupted by the arrival of Elkanah's students, young men full of life and energy, older and more experienced than Oren and Eitan. They looked up to Elkanah with respect and a desire to learn, watching his every move, absorbing every lesson he had to offer.

However, this calm was quickly shattered by a man who came running, his face pale. "The Philistines!" he panted, his words a desperate rasp. "They are attacking from the east! We need help! Elkanah, they need you!"

Fear instantly filled Hannah's heart. *Eitan. Oren.* They were at training today. *Lord, protect them! Be a shield of protection!*

In a moment, everything around Hannah turned into a flurry of hurried movements and grim faces as Elkanah and his students prepared to face this enemy.

The weight of worry and fear dropped like a rock into her heart. She again silently prayed for the men's safety and strength. She murmured quiet pleas to the heavens, asking for protection. Pleading for every man and boy to come home alive.

One of the musicians, a young man with a fiery temper, complained bitterly. "Why should we risk our lives for them? Let them fight their own battles!"

Elkanah silenced him with a stern look. "We are all brothers," he said firmly. "We must stand together."

More quickly than she could have imagined, the sounds of men preparing for battle filled the courtyard—the clatter of weapons and the cacophony of voices. But all she could hear was the silence where the music had been, a haunting void that echoed with the loss of something precious.

Elkanah approached her with quickened steps. He spread his fingers over her abdomen, and his lips moved quickly yet silently. Emotion knotted in Hannah's throat as she understood. Elkanah prayed a blessing over this child in case he did not return home.

Elkanah stepped back. His eyes were filled with determination and love. "I must go, Hannah," he said softly. "I must do what is right. I will find my sons, and we will fight together—they are no doubt already headed out to face the enemy."

She nodded, knowing she could not hold him back any more than she could hold back the welling tears. She could only pray for his safe return and for the return of all those who went with him, especially for Eitan and Oren.

As Elkanah strode out, the courtyard seemed to shrink, the world closing in around her. The instruments lay abandoned, their melody muted, leaving Hannah to face the profound truth of life's delicateness, its susceptibility to the whims of fate.

In Shiloh Hannah had faced the enemy of her soul. Now it was her husband's turn to fight the physical enemy—the one who threatened their very lives.

CHAPTER TWENTY

⬩—————⬩—————⬩

The air was laden with the scent of herbs and healing ointments as Hannah stepped into the dim chamber. Peninnah was seated beside Eitan, her complexion pallid. Her gaze, however, seemed to be focused more on Hannah's swelling stomach. *Out of curiosity or out of worry?* Hannah wondered. Probably both.

Peninnah stared, but she did not speak. Hannah chose to focus on the son instead of the mother. Today was not the day to allow Peninnah to bother her, not when she still did not know the details of where her husband and Oren were. She supposed not receiving news that they were injured or killed was the best she could expect during times like these. More important was that the men stay and protect the borders of Ephraim, lest the Philistines attempt to invade again.

Despite the shadows of pain etched on his countenance, Eitan's eyes flared with recognition as Hannah neared. A ripple of concern and a silent dialogue seemed to pass between him and his mother. Peninnah abruptly excused herself, leaving the room with a last lingering glance at Hannah's form. Eitan seemed unperturbed by his mother's sudden departure, perhaps understanding her unspoken emotions and internal conflicts as a second wife.

Hannah gently took Peninnah's vacated place by Eitan's side, her heart sending a silent prayer for the departing woman. She prayed for peace and strength for Peninnah, for her well-being, and for her own understanding of the silent battles she faced. Hannah's hand tenderly replaced Peninnah's on Eitan's, hoping to convey reassurance.

"Hannah." Eitan's mature yet fragile voice broke the silence, his body straining to find a better upright position. He seemed more man than boy now at fifteen, not just in stature but also in countenance, a reflection of the harsh realities he had witnessed, the cruelties of battle he had faced far too early.

"No, please do not try to sit up on my account." She leaned forward, bringing her face closer to his line of sight, her eyes probing his, searching for untold stories and hidden pain. "But you must tell me... Eitan, what happened?" Her voice trembled. Questions about his abba and brother lingered on the tip of her tongue, a cascade of concerns and unshed tears, but she held them back, not yet ready to release the floodgates until she knew the truth.

Eitan swallowed hard and took a deep breath. "We were in the hilly area, near the woods. We never expected the Philistines to attack from there. Their warriors came suddenly, emerging from the trees."

The tremor in his voice betrayed his attempt to sound brave. "They were so tall, Doda Hannah, like giants. With their bronze helmets gleaming in the sunlight and their spears... They seemed invincible."

She reached forward and gripped Eitan's hand tightly.

Eitan continued, "I tried to defend myself, using the rocks and trees for cover. But one of them… He was massive, towering over me. He swung his sword, and I barely had time to react. I managed to dodge, but not entirely. That is how I got this." He gestured weakly toward his injured arm, now swathed in strips of cloth, each one stained with blood, the vivid reminder of the encounter. "I succeeded in a partial evasion, but the blade found its mark nonetheless."

Their servant, Shifrah, had told Hannah that when he had first arrived, the bandage was a rough contrivance, hastily done in the heat of battle. And even though the wound had been cleaned and the bandages changed, his arm lay limp.

Hannah touched his forehead gently. "You are brave, Eitan. Yahweh was with you, or it could have been much worse."

Eitan nodded, and a tear ran down his cheek. "I have never felt such fear, Hannah. The stories we heard of their might, their stature… Seeing it firsthand, it was… It was overwhelming."

She offered a gentle smile, trying to give some solace. "It is all right to be afraid, Eitan. But you survived, and that is what matters. You are here with us now.'"

Along with the burden of newfound maturity, Eitan's face bore the etched lines of exhaustion, the shadows under his eyes telling tales of unrelenting fatigue and pain. She rose, ready to leave him to his much-needed rest. But as she moved, Eitan's eyes held a lingering shadow of unspoken words, a flicker of something he wanted to convey.

He seemed to wrestle with his thoughts for a moment and then broke the silence. "Don't worry about Abba and Oren," he said, his voice a fragile whisper. "They are looking out for each other." He paused as if gathering the remaining fragments of his strength. "Abba wanted me to give you a message. If the baby comes before he returns, he wishes for him to be called Samuel. It means 'God hears.'"

Hannah nodded as relief, worry, and gratitude weaved within her. "Thank you," she managed, emotion constricting her voice. She cleared her throat and tried once more. "Thank you for delivering that message." She placed her hand on her taut, round belly, silently praying she had weeks, not days, before Samuel arrived. She bid Eitan a quick recovery and goodbye and left him to sleep.

Hannah had just returned to her side of the dwelling when a sharp, sudden jolt of pain seized her belly, a jolt of unexpected agony. She cried out and clutched her stomach. Panic engulfed her like an icy wave, dark tendrils of fear rooting deep within her heart. She questioned the reality of the moment, her breath caught in the mingling of pain and fear. Had the awaited time finally arrived?

With tentative steps while wincing in pain, Hannah moved to the courtyard, a place usually vibrant with the hustle of daily life, now a silent backdrop to her travail. The air around her seemed to tighten, the texture of the surroundings intensifying with her heightened senses. "Shifrah!" she called out, her voice breaking, cracking the air with its terror-filled note. She needed the servant to find Deborah, who had delivered all of Peninnah's babies. "Shifrah, please come!"

Her calls met with no response. A sudden realization hit her. They had gone to the field to harvest as much as possible. It was a bit early in the season but necessary, a precaution against the looming threat of the Philistines destroying their crops, which would lead to a harsh and hungry winter.

Peninnah appeared in the doorway, the color drained from her face, eyes widened and laced with concern. "Hannah, what is wrong? The baby?" She rushed to Hannah's side and put an arm around her to steady her.

Hannah's breath came in ragged gasps. Another pain hit her. "Something is wrong." The air felt thick and heavy, the usual sounds of daily life and nature paused, amplifying her pain and fears.

"I will fetch Deborah. But we may not have time." Peninnah's voice trembled, the uncertainty clear. "Babies sometimes come so quickly."

Hannah pressed her lips together. She tried to process Peninnah's words as the tightening of her abdomen took her breath away. "How do you know…" The question began to form on Hannah's lips, but realization stifled it. Of course Peninnah knew. She had birthed many children for Elkanah, facing the mighty waves of pain time after time. Another spasm gripped Hannah, forcing her back to arch and a stifled cry to escape.

Through the haze of her pain, Hannah glimpsed Peninnah's face, which was marked by knowledge and sympathy. Every surge of pain pushed her closer to a deeper connection with Peninnah, revealing the intricacies of their shared journey.

"I cannot lose this child, Peninnah," Hannah whispered, tears in her eyes. "I cannot."

"You will not," Peninnah assured her, her voice strong and determined. "We will get through this together. I know it hurts, but your body is simply doing what it was designed to do. Relax, Hannah, as much as you can, and allow your body to do its work."

Another wave of pain hit Hannah, even more intense. She cried out, her body writhing in agony. Peninnah helped Hannah to settle and then checked the baby's progress.

"The good news is that it does not appear the baby is quite ready yet." Peninnah's face tightened, and her eyes filled with determination. "I am going for the midwife."

CHAPTER TWENTY-ONE

———— ◆ ———— ◆ ————

Hannah lay on the mat, body aching and forehead slick with sweat. The loom in the corner stood unused, a focal point for her during each wave of pain. It symbolized the life and future of her unborn son, still in the process of being woven by God's hand.

Sitting in the room's shadow, Deborah, the seasoned midwife, watched over Hannah. Her gnarled hands never stopped their ceaseless motion, grinding herbs with an age-worn pestle in an equally old mortar. The resultant pulp, a greenish concoction, was then applied to linen, ready to soothe Hannah when the pains grew more intense. The bitter smell of the herbs tinged the air, a potent promise of relief.

Clay pots and utensils were arranged neatly around her, and outside, the sounds of sheep and haggling voices seemed distant and unrelated to her current state. Though the pain was intense, thoughts of her child fueled Hannah, compelling her to continue.

The arrival of footsteps reverberated in the confined space, the distinctive scuff of sandals hinting at a man's presence. When Hannah opened her eyes, Elkanah was there. He'd returned home in time for the birth of his son! He was wiping her forehead with his rough yet tender hand. His presence was comforting, his words soft and encouraging, soothing her strained senses.

Elkanah sat down beside her and took her hand. It was a small gesture, but it was everything. His touch was a statement, a vow, a commitment that needed no words. It was about them, their shared life, and the future that was about to unfold.

In the embrace of their humble dwelling, each moment was a whispered eternity of being, waiting. A sacred stillness enveloped their space. No hurried breaths, no echoes of urgency.

Yet after more hours passed without the arrival of their son, Elkanah paced the room, his face showing a battle between excitement and concern. He sometimes paused to press a cooling cloth to Hannah's forehead or to offer words of encouragement.

The bare walls of their home, usually a comforting familiarity, now echoed the scuffs of Elkanah's sandals against the earthen floor, a rhythmic drone accompanying the high pitch of the distant marketplace. Deborah had set up a small fire in the corner, and now the scent of olive oil and herbs grew stronger with each passing moment, wafting up from a simmering pot that sent curls of steam into the air, tendrils reaching up to the wooden rafters overhead.

Deborah knelt by Hannah's side, her hands strong and knowing. She guided Hannah through each contraction, her voice soothing and calm. The floor was covered with clean linens, and Deborah had a basin of warmed water nearby. She used it to wash her hands and soothe Hannah's body, following the traditions and knowledge passed down through generations.

"You hold the strength of mountains within you, my love," Elkanah whispered, his fingers gently weaving through her damp tresses. "Our years of whispered prayers and silent tears are nearing fruition."

"I feel it, Elkanah," came her reply. "In the depths of my being, I know this child is destined to be the vessel of the Divine, a living testament to His boundless grace."

Hannah's mind drifted through the corridors of time, revisiting the nights spent with her knees pressed to the earthen floor, her prayers mixed with her tears. Her faith had grown stronger in the waiting.

Another pain hit, but this time it was different. Hannah sensed that Samuel would soon be in her arms.

She leaned on Elkanah, her hand gripping his. The pain was a fire—a searing, relentless force. Still, it was also a gateway to fulfilling her deepest desire.

Elkanah's concern radiated off him like heat from the noonday sun. His hand, rough from years of laboring, was soft in its ministrations as he gently wiped Hannah's forehead.

"I am here with you, Hannah," whispered Deborah. Her hands, instruments of strength and blessing, cradled Hannah's. "Yahweh is with us, guiding us."

"Yes, He is," she managed to say. "I feel the presence of Yahweh."

"And you are a vessel chosen to bring this gift of life into the world," Deborah whispered back. "You are doing well, Hannah. The head is emerging." Deborah's eyes darted to Hannah's face. "Just a little longer."

The moment arrived with one long push through the pain and then a cry, a new voice joining the world. Samuel was born, his body slick and red, his wails solid and healthy. Deborah quickly cut the cord with a sharpened stone knife and wrapped him in swaddling cloths, following the age-old custom of their people.

"And he is the gift of Yahweh," Deborah murmured, her hands gently cradling the newborn. "He is beautiful."

Hannah felt tears roll down her cheeks as Deborah placed the newborn child in her arms. Her son's soft body melded into her embrace. His tiny fingers curled around Hannah's.

"He is here," Hannah whispered, her voice full of wonder and gratitude. "He is really here."

Elkanah's face was radiant, his eyes tearful with joy. He reached out to touch his son, his hand trembling with emotion. The room was filled with a profound sense of peace, a divine affirmation of promises kept.

Deborah busied herself with cleaning, and then she prepared a nourishing meal, her experienced hands moving with practiced ease. The scents of freshly baked bread and simmering stew filled the room, a comforting and homely reminder of life's simple blessings.

Hannah's heart was full, her soul singing with joy. She looked down at Samuel, her son, her miracle, and knew that the Lord had heard her prayer.

"What shall we name him?" Elkanah's voice broke through Hannah's thoughts.

Hannah looked up into Elkanah's face. Her tears blurred her view, but she couldn't miss the sparkle in her husband's eyes.

She couldn't help but smile. "You have a name already chosen, do you not? Eitan told me."

Elkanah nodded. "Yes. I am glad he was able to deliver the message. I chose Samuel."

Hannah's gaze lingered on the small form of Samuel, her heart brimming with joy, gratitude, and love. Elkanah stood, his figure silhouetted against the window, the hills beyond painted with the shadows of grazing sheep. But his mind seemed to be traversing realms beyond the mundane—to a place filled with divine whispers and heavenly requests.

"You are a promise, a covenant," Hannah whispered to the baby, her voice a soft melody of love and dedication. "You are our prayer answered, our journey fulfilled." Her fingers gently caressed the tiny hand.

Elkanah looked back at them. His eyes, mirrors of the deep spiritual currents flowing through his soul, met hers. "He will be a light in our times of darkness, the instrument of God to turn His people back to Him."

As Hannah held Samuel close, feeling his small heart beat in time with hers, she knew that Elkanah was right.

CHAPTER TWENTY-TWO

The creaking of the door announced Peninnah's arrival. The rustle of her finely woven garments told Hannah she had been visiting friends. Weariness pressed Hannah's body into the bed, yet at the same time her heart felt so light she was sure that if it wasn't enclosed inside her chest it would soar like the birds that rode the currents outside her window.

Hannah pulled in a deep breath. The room held the scents of new life. Of motherhood. The lingering aroma of herbs used during childbirth mixed with the warmth of Samuel's skin.

Peninnah entered the room with an air of both curiosity and hesitation. However, instead of moving toward Hannah, she stepped to the side. Instead of closing the door, she left it open. A face peeked in. Eitan stood taller than his imma. He came in, his arm still in a bandage and a sling, but he seemed to be doing better. His presence added something special to the room a blending of happiness, pain, growth, and love. Yes, family love.

"May we come meet our brother?" His voice cracked.

Hannah straightened. "We?"

"Yes, all of us are here." Eitan glanced over his shoulder. "Well, not the baby, of course." He entered tentatively.

Oren followed with a chuckle. He nearly reached his brother's height. "Not true. Tobiah is no longer the baby anymore. Congratulations, Doda."

"Oren!" If Hannah could have leapt out of the bed to give him an embrace, she would have.

"He arrived just last night," Eitan explained. "And he has come with news that for now our borders are secured. He and Abba do not have to return."

The children clustered around and leaned down for a closer look.

Hannah adjusted Samuel in her arms, lifting him slightly for the children to see. Abiram, Zemir, and Ya'akov followed next. Finally, Shifrah entered with Leeba's hand in hers.

Delight brightened the faces of the children as they peered down on their new brother. Yet Hannah couldn't help but look to Peninnah. Peninnah's eyes, sharp and assessing, softened as they fell upon the tiny form of Samuel, wrapped in swaddling cloth. Hannah nestled the baby closer.

"May I see him?" Peninnah asked, her voice oddly gentle. She moved closer, and her children stepped aside to allow her to approach, like the parting of the Red Sea.

"Of course," Hannah replied, shifting to make room. The fear that Peninnah would taunt or belittle her joy was there, an old shadow in her mind, but she pushed it away. Peninnah had changed.

Peninnah approached, her face alight with genuine interest. She reached out, her fingers gently brushing Samuel's soft cheek. The baby cooed, his tiny hand grasping at the air.

"He is beautiful, Hannah," Peninnah said, her voice totally sincere. "Truly a gift from the Lord."

Hannah's heart swelled with pride and gratitude. "He is," she agreed, her voice catching with emotion. "He truly is."

The atmosphere in the room seemed to mellow. The rivalry that had once been a sharp blade seemed to dull, becoming a distant memory overshadowed by shared experiences and mutual respect.

Suddenly, the harmonious hums of daily life outside grew louder, signaling the approach of dinnertime. A voice—Shifrah's, clear and resonant—pierced through the room, coming from Hannah's kitchen. "Time for dinner. Come now, children!"

With a nod from their mother, the children rushed out of the room to wash up. As they raced down the hall, their feet pounded eagerly against the earth. Through the open doorway the scent of cooked food began to waft in.

"They are always hungry," Peninnah said with a sigh. "Just you wait." A soft smile brushed her lips, a silent acknowledgment of the bond they now shared, a bridge built over a river of tears and laughter, pain and joy.

Hannah responded with a gentle nod, her eyes crinkling at the corners as she savored this moment of peace and unity. The unspoken words between them floated in the air, like delicate feathers caught in a gentle breeze, hinting at forgiveness and something that might be newfound friendship.

Finally, Peninnah rose. "I should go," she said, her voice gentle. "But thank you, Hannah, for letting me see him. He is truly a blessing."

"He is," Hannah agreed.

Peninnah moved toward the door, then paused, turning back. "May the Lord watch over him," she said sincerely. "And you too."

"Thank you, Peninnah." Hannah smiled and then kissed the top of Samuel's head. "May He watch over us all."

Peninnah closed the door softly behind her.

Hannah sat in the quiet room, her heart full of complex emotions. The visit was unexpected but full of grace and understanding. She looked down at Samuel, her precious son, and knew the path ahead would be challenging and require sacrifice. But she also knew that she was not alone. She found strength and solace in her faith, love for her child, and an unexpected understanding of the woman she had lived with for so many years.

The world outside continued on, the sounds of life and community drifting through the open window. But a sacred moment had just unfolded, a connection forged, and a new chapter begun.

The door opened, and Elkanah entered. His eyes, filled with love and tenderness, met Hannah's, and a silent conversation of love and shared joy danced in their gaze. He approached and stood beside them and caressed the dark locks of Samuel's hair. Then he began to sing.

Close your little eyes beneath the moon's tender glow;
Let the whispering winds rock you gently to and fro.
In the arms of the night, may you find sweet rest
As the world holds you, for you are blessed.

Dream of fields and mountains, rivers so serene,
Of the whispering trees and meadows so green.
Sleep, my precious, under the stars' soft glow
While the whispering night sings songs of love and woe.

As Hannah heard her husband's song, she could feel the
weight of the sacred vow she had uttered, the promise that was
born from her tears and pleas to the heavens. Each day, with
the sun telling tales of new beginnings and the moon singing
lullabies of enduring love, the silent heartbeat of that vow
throbbed within her. Yahweh had given her this great gift, and
when the time came, she was to offer Samuel back to Him.

It was clear that Elkanah felt the vow too. It had become a
part of their beings, enmeshed with their spirits, making its
presence known in the silent moments of shared glances and
tender touches. The only question now was *when.*

The sun was setting, painting the world with shades of amber
and rose. Hannah stood by the window, her beautiful boy
cradled in her arms, his tiny breaths a gentle rhythm against
her chest.

She looked down at his cherubic face, his plump cheeks
flushed with sleep, his tiny lips parted in contentment. Her

heart swelled with love and pride and a sharp pang of fear. The thought of placing him in Eli's hands, of walking away from this precious child, was a torment she could hardly bear. Cracks in her resolve were forming, allowing doubt to creep in.

"Hannah?" Elkanah said softly. "You are very quiet. Are you thinking about…"

She looked up. "I cannot bear the thought, Elkanah. I cannot bear to give him over to Eli. He is so small, so innocent. How can I give him up?"

Elkanah reached out, taking her hand, his touch warm and reassuring. "I know, my love. But we made a vow. We promised to give him to the Lord's service. All the days of his life."

Tears welled in Hannah's eyes. "I know, Elkanah. I know what I promised. But I truly did not know how much it would hurt. I look at him, and my heart aches with love."

She looked into Elkanah's eyes, searching for understanding, for strength. She saw the worry in his face, the fear that she might break her vow. But she also saw the love, the unwavering support that had always been her anchor.

"And what will Eli do with a baby? A baby needs his imma."

Worry darkened Elkanah's gaze. Hannah guessed his thoughts. *Is she planning to break the vow?*

Her heart wrestled a moment more. No, she would honor her commitment, no matter the pain. "I will keep the vow. I promise that." The words rushed out before she could stop them. "I will nurse him, love him, care for him until he is weaned," she said, her voice strong with determination. "And then, when the time is right, I will give him to the Lord."

Elkanah nodded, his eyes filled with pride and love. "I know you will, Hannah. I believe in you and know that Yahweh will give you—and me—the strength to do it."

CHAPTER TWENTY-THREE

Hannah awoke abruptly, her surroundings shrouded in remnants of a dream that seemed all too real. The vision of leaving Samuel at the tabernacle infiltrated her slumber, making every moment laden with the weight of impending reality.

She glanced at Samuel, who was now two years old, lying beside her. His presence was a constant reminder of the vow, a commitment wrapped in faith and desperation. Every moment with him was one moment closer to the inevitable separation. Hannah rose and moved to the window. *Lord, give me strength.*

She returned to bed and fell into a fitful slumber, but both she and Samuel were awake early. She was just finishing breakfast when a sudden knock resonated on the door. Samuel ran and pushed the door open.

Ayala, her presence like a breath of fresh air, stood there. "There he is, my baby brother!" Ayala cooed, sweeping Samuel into her arms.

"And where is your little one?" Hannah asked.

"My imma has taken Sarah to see the small lambs," Ayala replied, her voice a soft murmur of reassurance, her eyes twinkling. "My imma is forever keen to teach the young. She believes children must learn about chores early, but I think she just enjoys the extra pair of helping hands." Ayala winked.

Hannah chuckled, sharing a knowing glance with Ayala. "Ah, perhaps. Teaching the young does seem to come with its conveniences."

"Yes," Ayala agreed. "Perhaps it is the imma's wisdom to cultivate little helpers while they still find joy in learning new things."

Samuel wiggled in Ayala's arms. She laughed, and the moment his feet touched the ground, he raced off.

"And how about Samuel?" She eyed her little brother, who was stomping in a mud puddle just outside the open door. "Has he started chores yet? I am sure he would love to learn to sweep or cook!"

"Oh, not yet," Hannah replied. Her son would be growing up helping at the tabernacle, in whatever ways Eli saw fit. "I suspect he will be more interested in running around and discovering than sitting and learning."

Ayala's laugh rang out, a joyful melody in the morning air. "Ah, the boundless curiosity of youth! Maybe we should learn from them. Imagine the wonders we could uncover!"

Hannah added her laughter to the mix. She hoped it didn't sound as hollow as it felt. Her daily time with Samuel at her side and in her arms was fast coming to an end.

As the women moved outside to watch Samuel chase butterflies, the world around Hannah seemed to hold its breath. Amid the sounds of buzzing bees and the delicate perfume of jasmine, the conversation turned to celebrating the Passover in Shiloh.

"I'm brimming with anticipation!" Ayala clapped her hands. "To embrace the warmth of loved ones. Sarah should enjoy it more this year. Last year, she cried because of all the commotion and unfamiliar people."

When Hannah did not respond, Ayala eyed her curiously. "Are you not going?"

Hannah bit her lower lip. Her heart felt torn between wanting to go to worship Yahweh and her reluctance to part from Samuel. "I will not be going," she revealed, trying to keep her tone light.

Ayala's brow creased. "Hannah, think of the joyous laughter, the exquisite flavors of the feasts, and the many brilliant smiles awaiting us there! Samuel is old enough to go."

"No." The word blurted out. "Not this year." She forced a smile. "I am not a young new imma, remember. I cannot keep up." The ridiculous excuse tumbled out.

Ayala clasped Hannah's hands. She squeezed them with warmth and an understanding and peered deeply into Hannah's gaze, her eyes holding worry and questions.

"Hannah," Ayala said softly, like a gentle wind, "is it the fear for Samuel that is stopping you from wanting to go to Shiloh?"

Hannah's heart skipped a beat. Ayala did not know about the vow, she was sure of it. No one did except Hannah, Elkanah, and Yahweh Himself. Yet Ayala's question hit the mark nonetheless. Tears filled the corners of her eyes, and she quickly looked away. "It is hard to explain." No, the truth was that it was *impossible* to explain, but soon she would have to. But surely not until next year. Samuel was not yet weaned. She clung to that fact.

Ayala offered a compassionate smile. "I do understand, Hannah. Since Sarah came into this world, my fears have surfaced like never before. But Simeon is always there to remind me that our God, Yahweh, is our Protector and the Keeper of all Promises."

Promises. Hannah absorbed Ayala's words, each syllable sounding like the ring of a gong in her heart. "I will ponder your words. I will converse with my heart and seek the whispers of Yahweh."

Then, with a smile, she continued. "It seems the tables have turned, doesn't it, Ayala? I remember a time when I was the one reminding you of Yahweh's truths and sharing His word."

Ayala chuckled. "Indeed, times have changed! It appears I have learned well from you," she responded, her eyes sparkling with joy and shared memories.

Hannah joined in the laughter, the sweet sound mingling with the whispers of the breeze around them. "It seems so. You were a good student, absorbing the teachings of Yahweh."

The playful banter and smiles were like rays of sunlight piercing Hannah's clouded heart. Pulling a small cloth bag from the pouch tied around her waist, Hannah asked, "Would you help me plant the seeds for the garden herbs?"

"You know, for all the complaints I make about chores, there is something about this one, making a garden, that brings me joy. It is such a simple, pure happiness."

As they talked, their hands were busy with the earth, feeling the cool soil and dreaming of the fresh green leaves in a few weeks. The act of planting, of placing a tiny seed into the ground, was like a small prayer to the earth and to the heavens, a hope for growth and life and new beginnings.

"I promise to be there next year," Hannah finally said. She would have to be.

Ayala's gaze met hers, a mirror reflecting both understanding and quiet encouragement. "And we shall receive you with joy-filled hearts and embracing arms."

Just then Samuel came running. Hannah leaned down and opened her arms to him. His tiny arms wrapped around her neck. He smelled of the sun and the earth, a sweet fragrance of youth and freedom. Hannah lifted him, enveloping him in a tight, loving squeeze. From today on, she would remember every touch, every babble, as if it were the last one. Soon she would need these memories to sustain her the rest of her life.

The seeds, now planted, awaited the gentle touch of the rain and the loving kiss of the sun to burst into life. As Ayala said her goodbyes, Hannah cast one last look at the morning sky adorned with white puffs of clouds. She sent up a silent prayer for blessings and shields, for her precious Samuel, for her beloved Ayala, for the planted seeds and the harvest they would yield, and for the strength to do what was right when the time came.

Holding Samuel close, she stepped inside, the door closing softly behind. Hannah snuggled her son, breathing in the scent of his neck. One more year to be this boy's mother. She would not waste a moment of it.

Hannah sat near the window, the gentle evening breeze rustling through the olive trees, crickets filling the air with their song. The world was bathed in the moon's soft glow, a serene and intimate setting that invited reflection and remembrance.

Elkanah approached. "Hannah, everyone is packing to leave for Shiloh tomorrow. Why do you not come with us?" His voice was filled with genuine worry.

"As soon as the child is weaned," she replied, her voice a steady stream amid a storm of emotions. "Next year.

"Shiloh holds so much of our beginnings," she continued. "It is where our lives truly started weaving together." Her voice was gentle as she found solace in the distant horizon. "You were so much older, and I still felt like a child." It was not easy for her to talk about taking Samuel to Shiloh, so she steered the conversation to more nostalgic shores, to fond remembrances. "I remember when you first approached my abba about marriage. I was so young, so naive. Back then, it seemed almost like a dream that a man like you would want to be with someone like me."

Elkanah reached out and took her hand in his. "I saw something in you, Hannah," he said. "I saw your dedication to the Lord. I knew then that you were the woman I wanted to spend my life with."

Hannah looked at him, her heart full of love and gratitude but also a hint of despair, a shadow of the truth that hung over them like a silent specter.

"I know you will fulfill your vow," Elkanah continued. "I trust that the Lord will speak to your heart and tell you when it is to be fulfilled. I have faith in you, Hannah, and know you will do what is right. Until then..." Elkanah smiled, his eyes awash with love and tenderness. "I love to watch you care for our son. I always knew you would be a wonderful imma."

Hannah's heart swelled at his words. She looked down at their son, sleeping peacefully in her arms, his tiny face a picture of innocence and trust.

"I love him so much, Elkanah," she whispered. "I love being his imma. I love watching him grow, learn, and discover the world. It is everything I ever dreamed of and prayed for."

Elkanah brushed a tear from her cheek. "I know, Hannah. I know. And I know the Lord understands your heart, your love, your sacrifice. We will fulfill the promise together, with faith and trust in His plan."

They sat, hand in hand, bound by love and faith, by promises made and promises yet to be enacted. Hannah found strength in their bond, the deep and abiding love that would see them through the challenges to come.

CHAPTER TWENTY-FOUR

Hannah and Elkanah watched their three-year-old boy, who lay sleeping blissfully on his sleeping mat. He was unaware of the momentous decision that weighed heavily upon their hearts. Hannah couldn't tear her eyes away from him, this child of her longing, her miracle. She reached out to brush a stray lock of hair from his forehead, the soft texture of his skin a tangible reminder of her love and duty.

"What was I thinking?" she whispered, her voice revealing her confusion and doubt. "How can I turn my son over to Eli? His sons are still corrupt. The tabernacle is a place of sin and disgrace. How can I trust my child to such an environment?"

"You made a vow, Hannah," Elkanah reminded her gently, his voice tinged with sympathy. "And you know as well as I do that vows to the Lord are sacred. That is why I did not cancel it when I could have."

Even though he was trying to say the right thing, worry lines creased his brow. "We have a son because of your prayer, Hannah. And even when Samuel is in Shiloh, he will still be our son."

"But what if I am wrong?" Hannah's voice broke as the tears came. "What if I am sacrificing my son to a place that will lead him astray? What if I am failing him as an imma?"

Elkanah's voice was quiet when he finally spoke, his words carefully chosen. "To whom do we dedicate our son, Hannah? Is it Eli?"

The question hung in the air, a challenge and an inquiry wrapped into one. Hannah's hands trembled as she looked down at the child, her son, the one Yahweh had chosen to give her.

"No," she replied, her voice firm despite her fear. "It is Yahweh."

She looked up, meeting Elkanah's eyes, her mind full of a determination that surprised even her. "Yahweh chose to give me this son. He honored me, and I must honor Him, no matter the cost to me."

Elkanah's face softened, and he took Hannah's hand in his. "I know," he said simply. "I know."

They sat silently, their decision settling around them like a heavy blanket. The child continued to sleep, oblivious to the storm of emotions in his parents' hearts.

Hannah's mind filled with images of Samuel's future. Fear and doubt still gnawed at her. But beneath it all was a deep and abiding faith, a trust in the Yahweh who had never failed her.

She knew this was a test, a challenge she must face and overcome. She must be strong, not just for her son but for herself and Elkanah.

The room held the simple furnishings of their life—the loom in the corner, the clay pots, and the wooden utensils. But at that moment, it was also filled with something more profound, intangible, and yet as real as the child in her arms.

Hannah knew the path before them was fraught with uncertainty and danger, but she also knew they were not alone. Yahweh was with them.

With a glance at her son, a silent promise etched in her heart, she leaned against Elkanah, seeking and finding strength in his embrace. They were in this together, and they would see it through, guided by faith, driven by love, and bound by a vow that was as eternal as Yahweh, to whom it was made.

She was not alone. Elkanah's love and Yahweh's grace would guide her through this painful journey.

She picked up the sleeping child and kissed his forehead. "I will do this, my precious one. I will give you to the Lord. And I will trust that He will watch over you, guide you, and keep you safe."

As the sun dipped below the horizon, Hannah stood by the window, her son in her arms, her husband by her side. The world was bathed in a soft glow, the sight a moment of beauty and grace amid her heartache, pain, and resolution.

At that moment, Hannah knew she had the strength to do what she had promised.

The day had come. Samuel, her precious boy, was weaned, and the time came to fulfill her vow to the Lord. Her steps were heavy with purpose and sorrow as she prepared for the journey to the house of the Lord at Shiloh.

Along with a three-year-old bull, an ephah of flour, and a skin of wine, she took Samuel, his hand clasped tightly in hers, his young face full of innocence and excitement. He was of course too young to understand the significance of what was about to happen.

The journey allowed plenty of time for silent reflection. The landscape was a blur as Hannah's mind lingered on the moments of Samuel's childhood, the joy he brought her, and the promise she had made to the Lord. Elkanah walked beside her, a pillar of support.

When they arrived at Shiloh, the tabernacle loomed large, both inviting and imposing, a testament to the grandeur and mystery of the Almighty.

They slaughtered the bull, its life offered as a sacrifice, a symbol of Hannah's own offering. She watched as Eli performed the rituals, his movements practiced and reverent.

Then came the moment, the moment she had prayed for yet feared. With Samuel beside her, she approached Eli, her voice catching in her throat as she spoke, "Oh, my lord! As you live, my lord, I am the woman who stood in your presence, praying to the Lord. For this child I prayed, and the lord has granted me my petition that I made to Him. Therefore I have lent him to the Lord. As long as he lives, he is lent to the Lord."

Eli's eyes widened with recognition then softened with compassion as he looked down at Samuel. He laid a gentle hand on the boy's head, blessing him.

Samuel looked up at Eli with curiosity.

He does not know. He does not know that I am leaving him.

Hannah looked down at Samuel's innocent face, full of trust. Hannah's heart ached with love and a piercing sorrow.

Yahweh, I do not understand. Why does doing what is right often bring pain? She thought of the stories of her ancestors. It seemed those Yahweh used greatly also had to suffer the greatest losses. How often had she listened to Elkanah's stories and focused only on the victories? Her path was righteous, but it was not without pain.

The little boy, oblivious to the weight of his imma's sacrifice, reached up and grasped her finger. She had prayed fervently for this child, her heart's desire, and now she was bound to a promise that would separate them. Her commitment to Yahweh was unwavering, but it did not ease the tight knot of emotion in her throat.

After kissing Samuel's forehead, Hannah whispered, "I will always love you, yet I have strength because I know Yahweh loves you even more."

She wanted to speak words of faith but could not. The tears would flow and be impossible to stop.

Even though the tabernacle was tainted by the misdeeds of Eli's sons, Hannah found a sliver of peace, a gleam of hope in the knowledge that someone more powerful, more righteous resided there. In His boundless glory and divine majesty, Yahweh dwelled in the tabernacle too. His presence was a sanctuary, a refuge from corruption and decay. Her son, her precious Samuel, would abide and grow under the watchful eyes of the Divine.

This knowledge brought a cascade of joy to her soul, a reservoir of peace to her anxious heart. The divine presence, the sacred assurance, would see her through the impending storm of separation, the inevitable pain of parting. Her trust in Yahweh became her anchor, her faith the shield against the torrent of her heartache.

Yahweh had given her the chance to be a mother. Samuel was her miracle. Maybe her son would be a miracle here too. Perhaps he was Yahweh's instrument to bring about change in His holy place.

Hannah released Samuel and stepped back to see Elkanah standing beside her. She dared not glance at his face. To do so would cause her to burst into tears. With a final hug, a lingering look, and a prayer for strength and guidance, Hannah dropped her hands to her sides.

Samuel's innocent laughter rang in her ears as she stepped away, a sound that would echo in her heart forever.

With Elkanah's arm around her, she looked back one last time at where she had left Samuel, her soul overflowing with love, loss, and enduring trust in the Lord's plan. Yet Hannah had barely made it into a courtyard when something stirred within her. And as clearly as she had known that the child she'd carried was a son, she knew that Samuel would be the next great leader of Israel. Eli and his sons had brought sin into the tabernacle, yet Samuel would be the one to lead the people toward obediently loving Yahweh.

Hannah paused her steps in a moment of profound connection. Not concerned with the world around her, indifferent to the eyes that might be watching, she lifted her arms in a silent offering, a visible surrender.

Her voice rose in worship to Yahweh. It wove through the air with threads of gratitude and adoration, creating a tapestry of divine love and human devotion and praise.

My heart exults in the Lord; my horn is exalted in the
  Lord.
My mouth derides my enemies, because I rejoice in Your
  salvation.
There is none holy like the Lord: for there is none
  besides You;
There is no rock like our God.
Talk no more so very proudly, let not arrogance come
  from your mouth;
For the Lord is a God of knowledge, and by Him actions
  are weighed.
The bows of the mighty are broken, but the feeble bind
  on strength.
Those who were full have hired themselves out for
  bread,
But those who were hungry have ceased to hunger.
The barren has borne seven, but she who has many
  children is forlorn.
The Lord kills and brings to life; He brings down to
  Sheol and raises up.
The Lord makes poor and makes rich; He brings low
  and He exalts.
He raises up the poor from the dust;

He lifts the needy from the ash heap to make them sit
    with princes
And inherit a seat of honor.
For the pillars of the earth are the Lord's, and on them
    He has set the world.
He will guard the feet of His faithful ones,
But the wicked shall be cut off in darkness, for not by
    might shall a man prevail.

A breeze stirred, carrying the faint sound of a child's voice, and Hannah's heart clenched. Samuel, her precious son, her gift to the Lord, was now left in the care of Eli. The journey back to Ramah would be quiet, but she would find comfort in Elkanah's embrace and solace in her remaining family. But a part of her would always be in Shiloh, her soul forever connected to the son she had given to the Lord.

CHAPTER TWENTY-FIVE

The soft gleam of the oil lamp bestowed a warm, golden hue to the room, gently caressing the baby nestled in Hannah's loving embrace, this being her fifth blessing since the divine gift of Samuel. The baby's tiny, delicate fingers curled around a strand of her hair. With tenderness enveloping her heart, Hannah pressed a kiss to the baby's soft forehead, and the little one's eyes fluttered open to the world around her. "Well, good morning, precious. Soon you will witness your very first sunrise," Hannah whispered with a smile.

She turned to Deborah and saw tears in the older woman's eyes, a mirror of emotions. "Thank you, Deborah, for helping me birth another child into the world. You have conducted yourself with grace and strength."

A chuckle vibrated through Deborah's frame. "You are bestowing praises upon me? Truly, it felt as though my role was minimal. Your strength and determination during the birthing were unparalleled, compared to previous times."

"During the birth of Samuel, I was acutely aware that I was bringing forth a life only to surrender him to Yahweh soon after. Although my heart found peace in fulfilling Yahweh's wishes, my other children will remain with me."

"Yes, and I am overjoyed you have a second daughter. She looks like her abba, don't you think?"

Hannah noted the little one's black eyebrows, furrowed as if in serious contemplation. "Yes, very much so."

"All those years with no children, and now six born." Deborah sighed as she cleaned the chamber. "And is it gone now—the ache of the barren times?"

"I wish I could say it is, but the truth is that the tenderness is still there. I would be lying if I said that I did not wish Yahweh had a different story for me. The heartache of those years is like dark threads woven into the tapestry of my life. Even with the bright threads woven in after the birth of more children, the shades of the past do not change. Yet the further I get from those days, the more closely I can see the beauty of Yahweh's hand at work."

The baby stirred, nestling closer to Hannah's breast. The little one released a sigh, as if she was also paying attention to Hannah's story.

Deborah laughed. "And do you have a name for this little one, Hannah?"

"Perhaps Tikvah." It was a male voice that came from the doorway. Surprised, Hannah looked beyond Deborah to her husband, who stood in the shadows. How long had Elkanah stood there? From the soft smile on his lips, Hannah knew he had heard all of their exchange.

Although Hannah's body felt weak from labor, her heart pounded with a strength she had forgotten existed. And even though strands of gray streaked her hair, Hannah's limbs felt as strong as they had when she was a young bride.

Elkanah approached, and they both turned their attention to the baby, marveling at the softness of her skin and the sweet smell of her hair. A feeling of peace settled over Hannah, a deep and abiding contentment she had never known. Her faith had been tested, but she had held firm, and now she was rewarded with the ultimate blessings.

"Hannah?" Elkanah's voice was gentle, almost hesitant.

She looked up and smiled, tears glistening in her eyes. "Yes, my love?"

He knelt beside her, his eyes locked on the baby. "She is beautiful," he whispered. "Just like her imma."

Hannah's heart ached with happiness. She reached out and touched his face, feeling the roughness of his beard and his skin's warmth. "We are blessed, Elkanah. Truly blessed."

He took her hand and kissed it. "Yes, we are."

They sat silently, the baby cooing, the world outside forgotten. Hannah cradled her sixth heavenly blessing. Her arms, once empty, were filled once again with the divine gift of new life, a reminder of Yahweh's grace and love.

Outside, spring was announcing its arrival, filling the air with the fresh, sweet scent of blooming flowers. The beautiful fragrances seemed to tell of the world's kindness and Yahweh's fulfilled promises.

Hannah was excited about the upcoming visit to Shiloh, where she would bring a robe to Samuel, a tradition she held dear. Last year, twelve-year-old Samuel was nearly her height. She was sure he would be taller this year. She looked forward to seeing him and hearing about his special connection with Yahweh, evident even in his youth.

Her heart, once broken with despair, was now awash with joy and gratitude as she looked at her baby. The soft sounds of the little one were like melodies of hope and divine love to her ears.

Elkanah stood beside her, a constant, loving presence. His voice, gentle as the spring breeze, said, "Hannah, who would have thought the Lord would shower us with such abundance?"

Each touch from Elkanah, each loving glance, connected their souls, a beautiful duet of shared faith and mutual love. "Our journey, with its prayers and hopes, has been a sacred dance, each step leading us closer to this moment of divine grace," she said.

Hannah knew there would be challenges ahead and that life was never without its trials. But she also knew she had found peace and happiness that would sustain her through whatever came. Her faith had brought her to this place, and she was grateful.

As she looked down at the baby, a smile playing on her lips, she uttered a prayer of thanks, a prayer of love and gratitude for the joy bestowed upon her and Elkanah. With each new blessing, their dwelling had truly become a home.

CHAPTER TWENTY-SIX

Five Years Later

Hannah stood on the fringes of the gathering, her eyes focused on Samuel, who stood tall and commanding amid the Israelites. The setting sun cast long shadows over Mizpah, bathing the land in an amber hue. The murmurs of the crowd, which once resonated with anticipation and tension, had stilled, replaced by an almost palpable reverence.

I have seen him evolve from the cherished boy I gave to the Lord to this man—a leader, the beacon our people have prayed for.

Samuel's voice resonated with authority and clarity, slicing through the tranquility of the evening air, echoing around the gathering. "If you are returning to the Lord with all your hearts, then rid yourselves of the foreign gods and the Ashtoreths and commit yourselves to the Lord and serve Him only. Let the Sovereign guide your paths, and His words illuminate your spirits. Let us usher our hearts in unison to the embrace of the Divine, bowing in reverence to His boundless love and infinite wisdom."

His words were a powerful testimony of divine insight and prophetic truth, cascading over the assembly like the waters of a purifying stream, seeking to cleanse the spirits and refresh the souls of the listeners. His profound connection with the

Lord was evident, every word laden with the weight of divine wisdom and divine love, aimed to steer the hearts of the people back to the sanctuary of God's embrace.

Both pride and humility swirled in her soul, and her heart strained with unsaid prayers and silent blessings for her son.

The gathered masses leaned in, their hearts and souls receptive to the young man who was their spiritual guide, their link to the Lord. His words were not just heard. They were felt. He was the shepherd leading his flock back to the sacred pastures of faith, reminding them of their ancestors' covenant with their Creator.

I gave him to the Lord. And I see the manifestation of God's promise in his growth. He urges our people to remember, return, and revere the God of our forefathers.

Her once tiny bundle, her Samuel, was destined to guide in their people back to the divine embrace, to be the vessel through which God would renew His covenant with His children.

His journey was not just his own but that of an entire nation.

With every heartbeat and breath, Hannah offered silent thanks to the Creator for allowing her to be part of His perfect plan for blessing her with the honor of being Samuel's mother.

As the threads of gratitude wove through her being, her five other children, the blessings who filled her and Elkanah's lives with joy and their home with laughter, approached. Each one, from fourteen-year-old Abijah to lively five-year-old Tikvah, was a testament to the Lord's kindness and boundless love, every smile a reminder of His enduring grace.

Peninnah's children were now all grown and married, with children of their own. Most had made the journey to Shiloh this year and were scattered about the encampment. Peninnah was no doubt helping to tend to the little ones. Hannah and Peninnah had come to a true understanding, and their friendship and respect for each other grew and deepened over the years.

Little Tikvah, with her tendrils of sun-kissed hair dancing around her cherubic face, broke away from her siblings and sprinted toward Hannah. Her small feet barely touched the ground as she ran, her laughter a melody of innocence and joy echoing in the tranquil air. Her eyes sparkling with youthful excitement, she reached up to clasp Hannah's hand, her fingers curling around her imma's with unwavering trust and affection.

A wave of warmth and love enveloped Hannah as she looked upon her youngest. She bent down, whispering sweet words. "My little dove," Hannah murmured, her lips brushing against Tikvah's cheek, "may the Lord continue to shower His blessings upon you."

Elkanah, with the soft smile that had won her heart all those years ago, joined them, the other children trailing behind him, their faces a mixture of curiosity and reverence. His hand found hers, his touch a silent promise of enduring love and shared destinies. "They wanted to see their brother, to witness the fulfillment of the Lord's promise."

The children, full of wonder, looked toward Samuel. His presence and words were seeds of divine wisdom being planted in their young hearts, sprouts of faith that would grow and weave through the fabric of their beings.

Hannah, with her family beside her, felt the waves of divine love and grace envelop them. In this moment of sacred union, of heavenly communion, she knew that they, her family, were part of a divine tapestry, threads in the intricate weave of God's boundless love and eternal plan.

Hannah observed as the people came closer to Samuel in a collective spirit of repentance.

"We have sinned against the Lord," they confessed, and Hannah's heart ached with the weight of those words. But amid that pain was hope, a promise of redemption.

As the assembly dispersed, Samuel's gaze met Hannah's. In that brief moment, no spoken words were necessary. He understood the sacrifice she had made and would honor his destiny, just as she had honored her vow so long ago.

With Yahweh's grace, all promises were fulfilled.

Letter from
THE AUTHOR

Dear Reader,

Looking closely at the Bible, we understand it's not just a collection of loosely connected stories but a tapestry of God's grand plans. No matter how minor a story may seem, it's an important part of the big picture of God's plan for His people. The story of Hannah is one of these that recently stood out to me in a new way.

At first glance, Hannah's story might seem like a touching tale of personal pain, victory, and fulfillment. But it has a much bigger meaning when you look more closely, especially in light of Israel's troubled history.

During Hannah's time, the land was rife with corruption and spiritual decay. The Philistines were always a threat, and Samson, the last judge, had died, so there was no one to lead the people. Instead of being spiritual leaders, the sons of the high priests added to the country's moral decline. It was one of the worst times in Israel's history. Still, as always, God had a plan.

Hannah comes along. She is a barren woman whose faith in God is strong. During Passover, she promises that if God gives her a son, she will dedicate her son to serving Yahweh.

This was not just the cry of a desperate woman. It was also a fervent prayer.

God heard. Samuel was born.

Hannah's devotion was not just for herself. It was also a sign from God. Samuel was not simply the answer to Hannah's prayers. He was also the answer to the prayers of a country that desperately needed a leader. Samuel became the last and one of the most important judges. He helped Israel change from a group of separate tribes to a united kingdom under the rule of Saul and David, the first two kings.

Hannah's story is like Mary's in the New Testament in many ways. In the same way that Mary's unplanned pregnancy made way for the Savior of the world, Samuel's miraculous birth changed the course of Israel's history. Through their faith and obedience, both women helped bring about important changes in the history of mankind's redemption.

When we hear stories like Hannah's, we are reminded how deep and wide the Bible is. Every story, character, and event in the Bible is part of a bigger, divine plan that comes to light as we read God's Word and ask Him for wisdom. God's stories teach us that in the big picture of life and history, no thread, no matter how small, is wasted.

I hope you enjoyed this story of Hannah. Also, as you continue to read the Bible, I hope you get deeper insights and revelations from Yahweh!

All the best,
Tricia Goyer

A SCHOLAR'S VIEW
OF SHILOH

Let's take a trip to Israel. We'll land at the Tel Aviv airport, rent a car, and head north toward the Palestinian West Bank. The hills are rolling, rather sparse, and filled with endless amounts of rocks. In his time there, David would have had no problem finding stones to fire at Goliath. Our destination is the town of Knirbet-Seilun, about nineteen miles north of Jerusalem near the Israeli settlement town of Shiloh and north of the Palestinian town of Turmus Ayya.

When we arrive in Knirbet-Seilun, we discover a quintessentially Palestinian village, featuring a main city square filled with shops selling everything from spices to shawls and robes. Merchants run out to greet us and offer their wares. Why have we come to Knirbet-Seilun? Because it is the living remnant of the Old Testament town of Shiloh.

A Westerner finds it hard to imagine that a settlement existed here at least 3,900 years ago. Remains from both the Canaanite and Israeli eras tell us that ancient Shiloh was a station on a sojourner's—temporary resident's—journey with little significance beyond a place in the religious history of Israel.

The first mention of Shiloh appears when Joshua and the Israelites entered the land and set up the tent of meeting inside the tabernacle, a designated area of the village. As the people gathered around the worship center, the land was divided among the twelve tribes. As the tribes set out to build their villages, Shiloh remained the religious hub of life in ancient Israel until David made Jerusalem the capital of the nation.

The Talmud indicates that the tent sanctuary and the tabernacle remained at Shiloh for 369 years. Scripture indicates that the tent remained holy to the Israelites, and they could expect to meet God there. From the time of Moses until the Temple Mount in Jerusalem, the people worshipped in Shiloh and held the tent of meeting and tabernacle in awe.

God had commanded that the tent be built with nothing but the finest materials. Gold, silver, and bronze were to be inlaid inside. Only the finest cloth of red and purple could be used. Inlaid with, spices, rubies, sapphires, and topaz, a wooden frame constructed from leather and covered by animal skins held up the structure of the tent. Inside, the walls were lined with tapestries, and a veil divided the tent into two sections. In the front portion, an altar held the offering bread. The Ark of the Covenant, the Holy of Holies, was kept behind the veil. The Ark, a golden chest, contained the two tablets of the Ten Commandments written by Moses, as well as reminders of the desert journey, Aaron's rod, and a pot of manna. On the top of the Ark were two golden cherubim and a mercy seat for God.

The tabernacle was surrounded by a large courtyard with linen curtains around the tent. An altar was stationed in the courtyard for burnt offerings. Nearby stood a large basin where

priests washed their hands. While the tent was not a permanent structure, the description certainly sounds impressive.

The promise to Israel was that the tent and tabernacle
would be the place where the Lord Adonai would dwell in their
midst (Exodus 25:8). When Hannah could not conceive, she
came to the tent of meeting because she was sure Yahweh
would hear her petition there.

What should modern people think of the entire situation?

The secular-minded person writes off the story as supersti-
tion and doesn't give it a second thought. The average church-
goer accepts the story as another ancient biblical account and
may give it little further consideration.

But the testimony of Scripture is clear. The Lord promised
to meet His people at the tent of meeting. And the Lord God
Almighty keeps His promises. Can we find a contemporary
analogy to express what happened to Hannah?

Possibly a present-day concept might help. We often speak of
portals when we want to describe an opening that uniquely car-
ries people to a different place and time. Football players can
enter a portal and be lifted out of one school and placed in
another university. A portal in space suggests breaking a time or
place barrier. Why not suggest that the tent of meeting was a special portal that took one from the natural into the spiritual realm?
Was this so for Hannah? She came to Shiloh barren and was soon
pregnant. Hannah went on to have six more children. Obviously,
her time at the tent of meeting was miraculous. A portal indeed!

Hannah's son Samuel was given to the high priest Eli when
he was possibly as young as four years old. The boy grew up in

and around the courtyard that surrounded the tent. We might wonder who cared for the child and how was he raised. While Scripture does not tell us many details, we know Eli had a wife, because he had two sons. We can surmise that she likely had a hand in caring for Samuel's basic needs. Scripture does tell us that Hannah and her husband, Elkanah, continued to make a yearly offering and sacrifice at the tent, and always brought Samuel a long loose robe to wear over his tunic. We discover that as Samuel grew, he served in the tent and wore a linen-lined ephod, a sleeveless close-fitting garment something like a pullover T-shirt. His life was totally devoted and absorbed with the ministry at Shiloh.

What could this child do around the shrine as he grew toward manhood? Sleeping in the tabernacle at night, he probably made sure the seven-branched golden lamps did not go out. He would have been the one who opened the doors of the tabernacle each morning, in addition to a multitude of other responsibilities.

Probably no one today uses the book of Leviticus in their morning devotions, so we're not in touch with the almost endless guidelines and commandments for how the ritual life of the Hebrews was to be conducted. Take a moment to glance through Leviticus, and you'll be amazed when you consider what a child must have done to make sure all the rules were followed. The failure to keep these directions came with a stiff penalty. Consequently, Samuel grew up in an almost monastic environment that must have shaped and molded his personality, thinking, and beliefs.

Behind the scenes stands the prophet Eli. We can't understand Samuel without his caregiver. Eli had failed with his two sons and seems to have ignored their debacles and crimes. By the time Samuel came, he gave studious attention to the boy.

Whatever Eli's failings, he raised Samuel to be a great man: Israel's last judge and first prophet. Hannah and Elkanah's personal sacrifice was not in vain.

Fiction Author
TRICIA GOYER

Tricia Goyer is an award-winning, bestselling author of more than ninety books, writing both fiction and nonfiction related to family and parenting. She is a frequent speaker at events and conferences, as well as a podcaster. Tricia loves teaching others how to write and get published.

A homeschooling mom of ten, including seven by adoption, Tricia is also a grandmother to many and wife to John. With a busy life, she understands the importance of making every word count.

Nonfiction Author
ROBERT L. WISE, Ph.D.

The Rev. Robert L. Wise, Ph.D., is the author of thirty-five books and numerous articles published in English, Spanish, Dutch, Chinese, Japanese, and German. On the internet he weekly publishes *Miracles Never Cease* and monthly presents live interviews on YouTube with people who have experienced divine interventions.

*Read on for a sneak peek of the first book in an exciting
new biblical fiction series from Guideposts Books—
Mysteries & Wonders of the Bible!*

UNVEILED:
TAMAR'S STORY

BY ROSEANNA M. WHITE

The girls chattered as they knelt before the huge loom in the weaving room. Tamar paced the floor along the length of the loom, watching every movement as fabric emerged from the intricately, perfectly woven cords. She barely heard their girlish talk, their voices blending with others that drifted through two wide windows. A nearly imperceptible breeze carried the aroma of onions and herbs from the market.

The scent almost distracted her. Last night the *Pesach* celebration had begun, and she'd eaten the first meal with her family. Her sisters and nieces would already be at work on the food for the second day of the weeklong feast, while she oversaw the last of the holy work they would do in the weaving room for the next week. No doubt her family was busy chopping the vegetables and herbs, gathering the eggs, while her cousin Levi, a priest in the temple, would be just as busy today as yesterday, slaughtering the lambs for the visitors to Jerusalem and gentiles who wished to celebrate with them. Levi, exhausted last night after the slaughtering for the resident Jews, had mused on how they might have to extend the Pesach sacrifices yet another day if the celebration grew any more.

Proof, they'd all agreed, that the Lord was at work in the world.

She jerked her attention back to the weaving room and the girls in her charge. Tamar smiled at their prattling voices, focusing on the fabric slowly growing on the cloth roll. She inspected the progress at each of the seventy-two rods with an expert eye to ensure every girl exerted the exact amount of tension needed. Their chatter quieted at her approach and began again as she moved along. She hid a smile. They weren't afraid of her, but they did respect her, especially the new girls— as they should for one who had served Adonai in such a sacred capacity for more than fifteen years.

Halting, she dropped to her knees. A wayward thread protruded from the tightly-woven cloth. She tugged lightly on the offending thread, and all conversation ceased.

"Did you not see this, Bithnia?" She looked at one of six girls who had joined the group two weeks before.

Bithnia's smooth brow puckered. She leaned across the taut rows of cords to examine the errant thread. "I…" She swallowed. "I did not notice. One of the strands must have frayed."

Tamar drew in a deep, calming breath.

"You *must* be more attentive." She controlled her tone but allowed a slight scold to creep in. She stood to look down on the girl. "One day this veil will guard the Most Holy Place. Adonai Himself ordained the design, and every strand *must* be perfect."

Bithnia rocked back on her heels, her head drooping forward. "Yes, Tamar. I...I was distracted."

"Distracted?" Tamar raised her voice to address the entire room. "This work is holy. We cannot become inattentive. This curtain is blessed. Sacred. It will safeguard the very presence of the Holy One. Who knows what might happen if the veil was imperfect?"

No one answered, the silence broken only by the sounds from the market.

Tamar bent, wrapped the strand around her fingers, and tore it from the woven fabric. She raised it, a scarlet thread to represent fire. When she knew she had everyone's attention, she released it. It fluttered downward and came to rest across the warp cords.

"Had we found it during the weave, we might have saved part of the veil. But now..." She drew in a deep breath and almost whispered, "Clear the loom and discard this imperfect fabric. We must begin again."

The girls raised a groan, and those around Bithnia glared at her. Tamar softened when the girl's features fell. She spoke, again loud enough to be heard, but this time with more compassion.

"Adonai knows we are not perfect." Again, the girls fell silent. Tamar gazed at the line of young weavers, each pair of eyes fixed on her. "That is the reason for the sin sacrifice, is it not?" The girls nodded, and Tamar smiled at Bithnia. "Did King Solomon not say, 'two are better than one'? We help each—"

A commotion from outside interrupted her. A cacophony of angry cries filled the air. Not market shoppers. This sounded more like a mob. Tamar approached the closest of the windows and leaned out to look down the narrow lane.

To her left she saw only the shops and buildings lining the street until the road curved at the top of the hill. She turned her head to the right, toward the market, and her breath froze.

People packed the narrow lane, most walking backward to watch whatever followed. Their voices roared, some wailing, some shouting, some cursing. Beyond them the metal helmets of Roman guards gleamed in the morning sunlight.

Tamar's stomach dropped. Another crucifixion.

She hurried to the door and threw it open then stepped onto the narrow stoop. Dimly aware that the girls stood behind her or huddled around the windows, she stood as a barrier between them and the swiftly approaching crowd.

The mob filed past, their garb identifying them as Jews. Probably pilgrims to Jerusalem, come to celebrate Pesach. But why were they so angry?

As the first wave passed, she heard the thudding of feet on the stone road. Through the crowd, she glimpsed a row of Roman soldiers, identifiable by their uniforms. And then...

Her stomach lurched. She'd seen crucifixions, but this man was barely recognizable as a man, his face so disfigured from the beatings he had endured. Blood streamed from a crude circlet on His head, and even from this distance she saw huge thorns digging into His skull. Just watching Him struggle to take His next step made her body ache.

"Who is that?" she whispered.

Tamar hardly knew that she had spoken until someone sniffled. She turned to find Bithnia standing beside her. Tears ran down the young woman's face.

"It is Jesus."

Work on the curtain progressed slowly. Tamar helped the girls remove the flawed fabric and drag it off to be discarded. They'd only been working on this veil for a few weeks, so the weight was manageable. Then they began the process of threading the tightly-woven warp through each rod, attaching the weight stones, checking each cord's tension while ensuring that the twenty-four strands were firmly wound.

She was bent over the eighth rod when the light failed.

The room was enveloped in darkness. One young woman squealed in fear, and soon half the others joined in. Though she understood their fear—even experienced some herself—Tamar straightened and spoke firmly.

"Girls, control yourselves. Davorah, Hinda, Illana. Bring lamps from the storeroom."

They hesitated only a moment but then moved as one toward the back room.

Tamar addressed the rest of the weavers. "'Tis a terrible storm, no doubt. It will pass. We've lost too much time on this veil already. We can't afford to waste any more." She forced a calm breath. "I know we all have Pesach meals waiting for us at home. Let us work quickly so we can join our families soon."

Though she heard several whimpers, Tamar ignored them and walked toward the door. She opened it and stepped outside.

The tall buildings that lined the street lay in deep darkness. It was around noon, but the sky was as dark as if it were midnight. She barely discerned the black clouds filling the sky. It seemed the sun had disappeared. From the marketplace came nervous voices, fear apparent in their cries.

She stepped back inside and turned to the seventy-two anxious women.

"As I said, a storm." She forced confidence. "Like all storms, it will pass."

The three returned from the storeroom. Tamar directed the placement and lighting of the lamps until the room glowed. The flickering lamplight soothed their nerves, and the sound of fearful sniffling disappeared. Work began again.

Hours passed. The girls worked diligently at preparing the loom for the new veil, Tamar inspecting every movement. At rod forty-two, Illana finished securing the warp and then moved to the next one.

Tamar stiffened. "Why are you overseeing two rods?" She surveyed the row of weavers and identified the missing girl. "Where is Bithnia?"

Illana bowed her head. "She left."

"Left?" Tamar drew a deep breath. One of the chosen weavers abandoned her post? "When did she leave? And why?"

Illana kept her head down. "When the sun darkened. She went to Golgotha."

The hill of crucifixions. The truth hit Tamar. "Bithnia follows Jesus."

It was not a question, but Illana answered anyway.

"She does. She said she could not stay here while…" The girl swallowed and risked a glance at Tamar. "While her *Messiah* is dying."

Tamar gasped. Who hadn't heard of this Jesus, the one claiming to be the Son of God? She herself had been swept up in emotions a week before, when the carpenter rode into Jerusalem on a donkey.

But to desert your sacred post? To leave the others to carry on your task? It was unthinkable!

She started to say so, but the words never came.

A loud rumble interrupted her thoughts. Tamar covered her ears to drown out the sound, but it seemed to reverberate from the soles of her feet up through her body.

The vibration intensified. The earth shook until it tossed Tamar sideways. She grasped Illana for balance, but Illana had none, and together they tumbled to the ground. Fear gripped Tamar. She grabbed her knees and curled into a ball, praying for the tremors to cease.

Though the earthquake ceased after only a few seconds, it seemed to last a lifetime. The girls were still huddled around the room when Tamar stood, stretched, and drew in a breath of dusty-tasting air.

"Is anyone hurt?"

She allowed the girls a moment to take stock of themselves and their surroundings and to relax enough to answer her. She studied the frightened faces. This day had held enough turmoil. She was tempted to send them home.

But divine duty came first.

"Now," she said, "let us continue our work."

The girls released a sigh, but in it Tamar caught the tone of relief. These girls needed assurance that all was well, and that she—Tamar—was in control.

They worked for perhaps half an hour.

Then the door burst open with a loud *bang*. The man standing in the doorway wore the garb of a priest.

Tamar looked closer and gasped. This man was none other than High Priest Caiaphas.

She halted her inspection of the loom and knelt. In the fifteen years she had been overseeing the weaving of the holy veil, the high priest had never visited the weaving room. Why would he now? Did his presence have something to do with the darkness and terrifying earthquake?

"Where is Tamar?" His voice held suppressed rage.

"I…" The word was weak with fear. She cleared her throat. "I am Tamar."

The high priest paced forward.

"You will come with me, woman." He gripped her arm and dragged her toward the door.

"I—" Tamar gasped with pain. "Of course. Where are we—"

Caiaphas trampled the carefully strung cords and the holy threads and pulled her behind him. Tamar cast a helpless last glance at her girls' terrified expressions before he dragged her through the door and down the lane.

Tamar struggled to match his pace, but she was no match for the high priest's long legs. Merchants stared, their compassionate gazes turning to judgment when they recognized her captor.

The temple was not far, by design. Three hundred priests were needed to transport each perfectly completed veil. The high priest dragged Tamar the short distance in a few minutes.

"My lord, where are you taking me?" Tamar's teeth were clenched in fear.

"Hush, woman," Caiaphas spat, and Tamar fell silent.

They entered the holy temple through the Beautiful Gate. They passed through the gate into the Court of the Women, and still, Caiaphas dragged her forward.

When they reached the Gate of Nicanor, which separated the Court of the Women from that of Israel and of Priests, she dug her heels in.

"I cannot enter the Court of Priests," she gasped.

Caiaphas turned a glare on her that froze the breath in her chest. "Do not speak to me, you sinful woman."

Such anger, such accusation, in his eyes. Tamar shrank from his fury and shut her eyes as he dragged her forward.

Then he released her. She wavered on her feet. Terrified of divine retribution for entering a forbidden area, Tamar stood statue-like, afraid to look, to move. She heard the sound of a door sliding open and smelled the incense.

"Look, woman!" Caiaphas's voice ground out, fury clear in his words. "Look what you have done!"

Though she could barely breathe, Tamar raised her head and opened her eyes.

What she saw stunned her.

The curtain—the one she herself had overseen and finished not a month past—lay before her, ripped in two from top to bottom.

She closed her eyes and shook her head. No. Impossible. The veil was a hands-breadth thick and untearable.

And yet there it was. Torn in two. And beyond it…

Tamar collapsed prostrate to the floor. *No!* No one could look upon the Holy of Holies and live.

Caiaphas's voice cut through her horror. "You have done this. You have exposed the Lord to the world!"

No! The veil was perfect. I saw every strand woven into place!

But the words would not come. Once again, she peeked at the torn veil and beyond. The Holy of Holies, the dwelling place of God Himself, uncovered to the world.

What had she done?

The world was chaos, and in the wake of it, Valerius wanted both to run home and make certain his family was safe and stand still, his gaze on the man who hung lifeless before him. His heart, if he was being honest, already sprinted toward the

Roman sector of Jerusalem, toward his precious Mariana and their two children.

Had the quake shaken their home as it had this hill? What if the walls had come crumbling down around them, over them? What if they were injured—or worse? His gaze searched the road toward the city, but other than clouds of dust filling the lightening sky, he saw no obvious destruction. Even so, his feet itched to run.

But duty held him rooted to the ground on this hill the locals called Golgotha, the Place of the Skull. Duty...and wonder, all focused on the man who now hung lifeless from the middle of the three crosses. He knew the man—Jesus of Nazareth. Knew Him better than he was generally comfortable admitting. He had followed His teachings for the last two years, albeit mostly in secret.

Surely the time for secrecy was over. Nature itself had responded to this man—darkness covering the world as He suffered, the very earth shaking in protest as He breathed His last. And yet...He'd breathed His last. Died. What did that *mean*?

"Surely this is the Son of God." Valerius had spoken the words aloud a few minutes ago, as he fought to keep to his feet on the bucking landscape. They'd been aimed at Longinus, at the observers gathered, at his own confused heart.

He was still learning who God was, had been learning it ever since he and his wife first moved to Israel so he could accept this post as centurion. They'd been here seven years already—long enough to see zealots rise and fall, to crush rebellions, to become dreadfully familiar with the hatred leveled on him by most Jews he passed, simply because he was Roman.

"Pagan dogs," they called him and his soldiers. And he could understand that. The Romans were the conquerors, the ones who had stolen the Jews' right to enforce their own laws, who kept them carefully pinned under the rule of Rome.

But they spat the same words at his wife and the two little ones who had been born here, who had never even seen their homeland, and *that* was unacceptable. People could call *him* anything they wanted. But sweet little Livia? Precious baby Felix? They were innocents. Roman by birth, yes, but Israel was the only home they knew. And he and Mariana were raising them to worship the one true God.

The attitude wasn't so different from the very ones the Romans held the Jews in—disdain. And that was why it had taken several years for him to realize that this God of the Jews was different from the gods of Rome, despite how similar His followers were to anyone else in their hatred and bitterness. To realize that the One they claimed was sole creator of the whole world and all who had ever dwelled within it was, by that very definition, *his* God too, if he chose to accept Him.

A God not of a city, not of a nation, but of the world. A God not of thunder or rain, of fertility or harvest, of war or music, but of *all*. A God who willed peace and harmony. A God who *loved* His creation.

Loved *him*. It hadn't been fathomable, when he'd first begun to study the ways of this people from his first post in Capernaum. Gods didn't love mankind. Some were generous, some treated humanity kindly, but *love* was what men were to give to them, expecting nothing in return but favor now and then. Mostly, people just prayed against the evils of misfortune and pain and poverty. Gods used men as nothing more than pieces on a gameboard, acting out their own desires and whims, which could change with the tide.

This God—the God of the Jews—was something different.

That was when he had declared his own war—a war on the prejudice of both sides. He had defied all expectations of his Roman upbringing and begun to seek out the devout Jews in Capernaum, where he'd been stationed before this recent promotion to Jerusalem. He'd asked for instruction in the way of the Lord, and he had even used some of his family's legacy to build a much-needed synagogue.

It had won him friends, there in Capernaum. Friends he missed every day, and certainly every week when he tried to learn more of God. Gentiles were allowed into the outermost court of the temple, yes, but no farther. And in Jerusalem, none of the priests or scribes seemed to have any interest in speaking with and instructing the handful of Gentiles who collected in that court every Sabbath.

Longinus stepped to his side, his spear still dripping with the blood and water of the supposed heretic. His hand, clutching the wooden shaft, trembled. "I owe you an apology, Valerius," he said. His gaze too was locked on the man whose death he'd just confirmed.

On another day, Valerius might have smiled. Of all the Romans in Israel, of all the centurions he served with in the legion, Longinus was the one he counted as his closest friend, yes, even when they'd lived twenty miles apart and saw each other only rarely. But that didn't mean Longinus had understood as Valerius stopped offering sacrifices to Jupiter and Apollo. Certainly not as he'd begun to follow the teachings of the unassuming Rabbi from a random backwater.

Valerius had tried for the last year, after his promotion to Jerusalem, to get his friend to see what his own heart insisted—the man was more than a teacher. Valerius and Longinus both came from Rome, the heart of an empire that spanned the world, the heart of education and learning. They knew teachers.

Teachers didn't heal the blind.

Teachers didn't cast out demons.

Teachers didn't raise the dead.

"Son of God." This time, as the words fell from Valerius's lips, they were more prayer than statement.

"I thought…I thought I would grant you 'prophet,' at some point. The Jewish definition of one, that is. Certainly not an oracle like the ones we know. But the very earth does not lurch at the death of a prophet." His friend wiped at his eyes, blinked a few times. "But I don't even know what that phrase means—*Son of God*. How does this one God have a son? How *could* He if He is so unlike Roman gods? If He does not have affairs with human women like Jupiter or Apollo did in the days of the heroes, how could a son even be conceived?"

"I don't know." Valerius had been struggling with that ever since Jesus had actually paused to hear his request, sent through those hard-won friends in Capernaum. Since He had granted him the healing that his servant Gaius had so desperately needed. Since He had praised Valerius's faith as greater than what He could find in Israel.

Valerius had known, as he'd rushed home after his messengers returned from intercepting the teacher and found Gaius not only out of danger but on his feet, laughing with Mariana and playing with Livia, that *prophet* wasn't a strong enough word either. He'd read the accounts of the Jewish prophets. They too had saved people from death, yes. But not by a mere word from miles away.

He hadn't known, then, what to call Jesus. Even now, the words that sounded right from his lips carried more mystery than answer. "I don't know," he said again, "but I intend to learn."

Longinus shook his head. "How? You've been learning their ways for years already, studying under whatever rabbi will allow you to. You've said it yourself—they have no more answers than anyone about the things this man taught."

Valerius was Roman, from the heart of the empire, the heart of education. He knew how to discover what he needed to know, once he'd landed upon the questions that he should ask. He would simply do what he'd done before, when he wanted to learn about God.

He'd go straight to the people who should know and demonstrate that he was their friend.

"His disciples will have the answers." He turned to the small knot of them under the Rabbi's cross, though what he saw only made him frown. The man had a dozen core disciples, and hundreds of others who followed Him too, wherever He went.

Yet the only ones beneath the cross were a few women and one young man.

He couldn't just stride up and ask the mourners for a lesson. One of the weeping women was Jesus's mother, he was all but certain. He couldn't intrude on her grief like that—he could only imagine how his own mother would feel if she'd witnessed his execution. Broken. Distraught. Undone. Certainly not ready to answer theological questions from a stranger.

His determination leaked out in a sigh. "Another day. We had better see to the other two as quickly as we can. I want to get home and make certain everyone's all right."

Crucifixions were not his favorite things, but he'd volunteered to oversee this one when he learned that the rebel Barabbas had been released and the teacher offered up in his place. Valerius knew very well that it was jealousy from the religious leaders of the Jews that had led to this, nothing more. The teacher, the man so much more than a teacher, had been guilty of no crime against either Rome or Israel. Valerius had wanted to be sure someone was present to deal respectfully with Him—and with the others too, for that matter. *Criminal* did not mean the men weren't still men deserving of that last consideration.

The legs of the two convicts flanking Jesus had already been broken, and without that meager support, life hadn't lingered long. Valerius waved a few of his soldiers over to help him lower each of the crosses and remove the men from the beams.

Relief and panic warred in his blood when he heard a familiar voice call out, "Master!"

He spun, gaze finding Gaius easily as the old man ran through the dwindling crowd. Trusting that his men would carry out his orders, Valerius strode toward the servant who had been with his family all his life, who was more father than servant. Who would be dead now, if not for Jesus's gracious word of healing. "Gaius?"

He'd seemed younger since his healing too. He ran forward with the vitality of youth, not limping slowly as he'd done two years ago. His face still revealed his age, but it was uncreased with pain or panic of his own, which allowed Valerius to relax the knot of his shoulders.

Gaius smiled. "We knew you would be worried. Mistress bade me run to assure you that we are well. The only loss in the earthquake was that old vase you always hated anyway."

Valerius breathed a relieved laugh. "No loss at all, then—and thank you. I was indeed anxious."

"Of course." Then Gaius's face darkened as he looked beyond Valerius, toward the central cross even now being lowered. The weeping from the women at Jesus's feet grew louder as one of them begged to be allowed to hold her son. "It is true then. I hoped, when gossip reached us midday, that they were mistaken."

"If only they had been." Valerius's voice sounded heavy to his ears, as heavy as it felt in his throat. Never before had he followed a teacher who met such a fate, but he was now one of thousands of people who would have to face the most horrible of questions.

What was one to do when one's leader was executed? Try to keep His teachings alive after Him? Or admit that His enemies had won and slink back into whatever else life had to offer? Forget all Jesus had taught?

But Valerius *couldn't* forget. How could he, when Gaius stood beside him, healed and whole?

Regret twisted his stomach. He hadn't even met Jesus face-to-face to request the healing—he'd been too ashamed, too afraid that the great Rabbi would refuse to see him because he was Roman. In that moment, when he'd considered striking out to intercept Him, it hadn't mattered that he'd made friends with as many of the Jews as he could, that he'd funded the building of a synagogue, that he'd learned as much as possible about the Lord God.

He'd been absolutely certain of his own unworthiness. Absolutely certain that Jesus would refuse him if he dared to ask for something as unheard of as His presence in a Roman household.

Gaius's face twisted in pain. "It should have been me."

"Pardon?" Frowning, Valerius followed his friend's gaze to the limp figure now being held by one of the women.

"*I* should have died. I've lived my life, I'm an old man. A sinner. So many things I've done that I regret! Yet the Lord spared me, through one word from Jesus. How, then...*how?* How is He the one who has died, while I still walk the earth? It isn't fair. Isn't right. He's never done anything wrong."

Valerius sighed and reached out to clap a hand to Gaius's shoulder. He hoped it conveyed encouragement, though if it did, it was only by the grace of God. Heaven knew he himself had nothing to offer. "I know exactly how you feel. And yet here we are, left to sort out what it all means."

"Sir?" one of his men called to him, arm lifted in a bid for his attention.

Valerius nodded his acknowledgment, squeezed Gaius's shoulder, and then let go. "You had better get home. Please assure Mariana that I too am well and that I will be home as soon as I can get away."

Gaius's mouth curved in a small, sad smile. "You know very well what the mistress will say to that, Master."

Despite it all, a chuckle warmed his throat. He'd been wary, he could admit it, when his family arranged the marriage to a woman so much younger than he, a woman who, upon first glance at her lovely face, seemed ill-suited to be the wife of a centurion. But he had relented, because it was what one did.

And it had taken mere weeks for him to realize how wrong his first impression of Mariana had been. She was in fact the perfect centurion's wife. Far from resenting the time his duties demanded, she was the first to encourage him to be the best, most attentive officer he could be. To care for his men, for his tasks, for his superiors. And yet he couldn't suspect her of simply wanting him out of the house and her company, because she always welcomed him home with the warmest of affection and excitement.

It had taken mere weeks for his wariness to melt into a love he'd never expected to feel. And now, eight years into their marriage, he did indeed know what his beloved wife would say—to any duty, but especially this one, that involved the care of the teacher in whom they'd both put their trust.

"She'll say that I should stay as long as I am needed to ensure the teacher is given every respect, even now. Especially now."

Gaius nodded. "Livia won't be as quite as understanding, of course."

This time his chuckle was brighter, as the image of his small, demanding daughter filled his mind's eye. Demanding, but only of their presence. That was all she ever wanted—the people she loved best to surround her. "True."

Gaius stepped away. "I will assure them you are well too. And confirm the sad truth about the teacher. If you need anything else, Master—"

"I won't hesitate to send someone with a message. Thank you, Gaius." As his old friend hurried away, back to the Roman quarter, Valerius strode toward the men patiently waiting for his instruction.

The strange darkness had faded into a dull gray light, yes, but he couldn't shake the feeling that it was still there. Surrounding them. Consuming them. A thick, suffocating darkness that snuffed out all the light. It closed in again when Gaius left, seeming to settle on Valerius's shoulders and wrap its fingers around his throat.

His gaze tracked to the man in whom he'd put so much hope.

The Son of God. *Dead.*

Where did that leave the rest of them?

A Note from
THE EDITORS

W e hope you enjoyed another exciting volume in the Extraordinary Women of the Bible series, published by Guideposts. For over seventy-five years, Guideposts, a non-profit organization, has been driven by a vision of a world filled with hope. We aspire to be the voice of a trusted friend, a friend who makes you feel more hopeful and connected.

By making a purchase from Guideposts, you join our community in touching millions of lives, inspiring them to believe that all things are possible through faith, hope, and prayer. Your continued support allows us to provide uplifting resources to those in need. Whether through our communities, websites, apps, or publications, we inspire our audiences, bring them together, and comfort, uplift, entertain, and guide them. Visit us at guideposts.org to learn more.

We would love to hear from you. Write us at Guideposts, P.O. Box 5815, Harlan, Iowa 51593 or call us at (800) 932-2145. Did you love *A Promise Fulfilled: Hannah's Story*? Leave a review for this product on guideposts.org/shop. Your feedback helps others in our community find relevant products.

Find inspiration, find faith, find Guideposts.

Shop our best sellers and favorites at

guideposts.org/shop

Or scan the QR code to go directly
to our Shop

If you enjoyed Extraordinary Women of the Bible, check out our other Guideposts biblical fiction series!

ORDINARY WOMEN OF THE BIBLE

━━━━━━━━━━━━━━━━━━━━━

From generation to generation and every walk of life, God seeks out women to do His will. Scripture offers us but fleeting, tantalizing glimpses into the lives of a number of everyday women in Bible times—many of whom are not even named in its pages. In each volume of Guideposts' Ordinary Women of the Bible series, you'll meet one of these unsung, ordinary women face to face, and see how God used her to change the course of history.

SAVANNAH SECRETS

Welcome to Savannah, Georgia, a picture-perfect Southern city known for its manicured parks, moss-covered oaks, and antebellum architecture. Walk down one of the cobblestone streets, and you'll come upon Magnolia Investigations. It is here where two friends have joined forces to unravel some of Savannah's deepest secrets. Tag along as clues are exposed, red herrings discarded, and thrilling surprises revealed. Find inspiration in the special bond between Meredith Bellefontaine and Julia Foley. Cheer the friends on as they listen to their hearts and rely on their faith to solve each new case that comes their way.

The Hidden Gate
A Fallen Petal
Double Trouble
Whispering Bells
Where Time Stood Still
The Weight of Years
Willful Transgressions

Season's Meetings
Southern Fried Secrets
The Greatest of These
Patterns of Deception
The Waving Girl
Beneath a Dragon Moon
Garden Variety Crimes
Meant for Good
A Bone to Pick
Honeybees & Legacies
True Grits
Sapphire Secret
Jingle Bell Heist
Buried Secrets
A Puzzle of Pearls
Facing the Facts
Resurrecting Trouble
Forever and a Day

Find more inspiring stories in these best-loved Guideposts fiction series!

Mysteries of Lancaster County

Follow the Classen sisters as they unravel clues and uncover hidden secrets in Mysteries of Lancaster County. As you get to know these women and their friends, you'll see how God brings each of them together for a fresh start in life.

Secrets of Wayfarers Inn

Retired schoolteachers find themselves owners of an old warehouse-turned-inn that is filled with hidden passages, buried secrets, and stunning surprises that will set them on a course to puzzling mysteries from the Underground Railroad.

Tearoom Mysteries Series

Mix one stately Victorian home, a charming lakeside town in Maine, and two adventurous cousins with a passion for tea and hospitality. Add a large scoop of intriguing mystery, and sprinkle generously with faith, family, and friends, and you have the recipe for *Tearoom Mysteries*.

Ordinary Women of the Bible

Richly imagined stories—based on facts from the Bible—have all the plot twists and suspense of a great mystery, while bringing you fascinating insights on what it was like to be a woman living in the ancient world.

To learn more about these books, visit Guideposts.org/Shop